OXFORD
UNIVERSITY PRESS

Blackstone's Police Sergean
Inspectors' Mock Examination Paper 2023

Pack 1

Contents

i. Acknowledgements   3
   Introduction to the Mock Examination   3
   Instructions for Completion   6

ii. Question Booklet

iii. Answer Sheet

OXFORD
UNIVERSITY PRESS

Great Clarendon Street, Oxford, OX2 6DP,
United Kingdom

Oxford University Press is a department of the University of Oxford.
It furthers the University's objective of excellence in research, scholarship,
and education by publishing worldwide. Oxford is a registered trade mark of
Oxford University Press in the UK and in certain other countries

© Oxford University Press 2022

The moral rights of the author have been asserted

First Edition published in 2004
Nineteenth Edition published in 2022

Impression: 1

Public sector information reproduced under Open Government Licence v3.0
(http://www.nationalarchives.gov.uk/doc/open-government-licence/open-government-licence.htm)

Published in the United States of America by Oxford University Press
198 Madison Avenue, New York, NY 10016, United States of America

British Library Cataloguing in Publication Data

Data available

Library of Congress Control Number

Data available

ISBN 978–0–19–288373–5

Printed in the UK by
Bell & Bain Ltd., Glasgow

Acknowledgements

I would like to thank all the team at Oxford University Press for their continued and highly professional support and assistance in the production of this product.

Above all, I thank my wife, Kate, for giving me the utmost encouragement and self-belief without which none of this would ever have happened.

Paul Connor

Introduction to the Mock Examination

Every single MCQ (multiple-choice question) in this mock examination is based on the syllabuses for the sergeants' and inspectors' examinations of 2023.

Whilst this mock exam offers a useful means to test your knowledge and understanding of the police promotion examination syllabus, the content itself should not be considered indicative of the 'live' examination. Each MCQ has been created from relevant material contained in the three-volume Blackstone's Police Manuals for 2023 (Crime, Evidence and Procedure and General Police Duties). These Manuals are the basis for both of the police promotion examinations that will take place in 2023. As a result, **whatever police promotion examination you are taking**, you can be sure that each MCQ in this mock examination is a valid test of your knowledge and understanding of the law as all of the MCQs will directly relate to the material that you have studied for the examination.

*'How can this mock examination be suitable for **both** sets of candidates?'*

It is important to highlight that the material studied by sergeants' and inspectors' candidates is **exactly the same** apart from the exclusion of the chapter dealing with Weapons (from the *Crime Manual*) from the inspectors' examination.

In order to make this examination relevant to both sets of candidates, there will be no MCQs asked on that chapter. At this point, sergeants' candidates may think that the examination is less relevant to them; but this is not so.

My analysis of the last 18 sergeants' examinations shows that the excluded Weapons chapter was worth an average of three to four MCQs per examination. Not being questioned on that solitary chapter does not make this examination any less valuable to the sergeants' candidates as it represents a small part of the examination process for sergeants' candidates. As you will discover, the scope of the examination is still huge and I have still managed to cover a great many subjects within the 150 MCQs.

As the range of the three Manuals is significant, I have set MCQs across a broad spectrum of the syllabuses; this makes the examination as fair a test of your overall ability as is possible. Some areas that have, historically, been allocated several MCQs in the exams have been treated in the same way in this mock, e.g. *'Drink, Drugs and Driving'* and *'Theft & Related Offences'*. This means that the mock examination is a reasonable reflection of the content of the Manuals.

A by-product of this approach is that some of the MCQs in the mock examination may appear to relate to obscure or rarely used pieces of legislation. Historically, this is the source of many candidate complaints about the examination proper and the reason for the often heard criticism, *'It's not based on reality'* which has been levelled year after year at the police promotion examination process. What candidates need to remember is that the examination is not about the 'reality' of day-today policing; it is a test of an individual's knowledge and understanding of the law contained in the syllabuses. These MCQs should not be treated with contempt just because a candidate has never dealt with a particular offence or feels that it is unimportant; any such approach would be unwise. Remember that the police promotion examinations are based on the sergeants' and inspectors' syllabuses and therefore everything contained within those syllabuses is potentially testable.

The distribution of the MCQs across the three Manuals is structured so that at no stage of the mock examination will you find yourself answering 10 MCQs in a row on Crime or Evidence and Procedure etc.

Importantly, the structure of the MCQs in the mock examination matches the structure of MCQs that you will face in the examination proper. You cannot accurately assess your knowledge, understanding and application of the law if you are not testing it in the same way as you will be tested in your examination.

The style of MCQs you will face in your police promotion examination will mirror the following:

> BREEN plans an armed robbery on a security van that regularly picks up cash at a local bank. He enlists the help of FISH and TODD who agree to actually carry out the armed robbery while BREEN waits for them at a rendezvous point. BREEN has no intention of taking part in the commission of the armed robbery itself. Unknown to BREEN, the security company has been 'tipped off' about the robbery and changes the day of collection so that the security van does not arrive at the bank. FISH and TODD leave empty-handed.
>
> Does BREEN commit statutory conspiracy contrary to s. 1 of the Criminal Law Act 1977?
>
> **A** No, BREEN has no intention of taking part in the actual armed robbery itself.
> **B** Yes, BREEN commits the offence as soon as he plans the robbery and before he enlists the help of FISH and TODD.
> **C** No, the commission of the offence is impossible because the security van would never arrive at the bank.
> **D** Yes, BREEN has agreed on a course of conduct that will involve the commission of an offence.

Finally, you will notice when marking the mock examination that 10 MCQs will be excluded from the marking process—this mirrors the marking process in your examination proper. In your examination, the 10 MCQs that perform poorest against a broad range of criteria (contrary to popular myth, *the sole criteria* these questions are judged against *is not* how many candidates answer the MCQ incorrectly) will be removed from the marking process. As analysing future candidate performance in relation to the 150 MCQs in this mock exam to obtain such data is not possible, 10 MCQs have been randomly selected to count as those 'poor performing' MCQs to ensure that you are marked out of 140 rather than 150 MCQs.

Now that you are familiar with how the mock examination has been produced and written, it is appropriate to consider the benefits of taking the examination: this is primarily to be able to assess your performance accurately. This can, in turn, help you in a number of ways:

1. It may highlight areas of weakness (e.g. your knowledge of General Police Duties may not be as good as you think it is).

2. It may highlight areas of strength (e.g. your knowledge of Crime may be stronger than you think it is).

A direct consequence of the previous two points is that the mock examination could help you channel your study/revision into more productive areas of your syllabus.

3. It is a good test of your ability to deal with 150 MCQs in a three-hour period. The pressure of dealing with an MCQ once every 72 seconds (the average time per question) can be intense. Will you be able to cope with it? Will you have to take steps to increase the pace of your MCQ answering in order to complete the exam proper? On the other hand, did you finish with a great deal of time to spare? If so, are you giving the MCQs enough thought before answering?

I cannot stress enough how important this benefit is. A friend of mine provides an all-too-familiar unfortunate but real-life case study. He sat the sergeants' examination but ran out of time with 20 questions left to answer; he did not even have time to guess the answers and consequently lost all of those marks. Unsurprisingly he failed the examination. Even if he had time to hurriedly answer the last 20 MCQs, this is a far from ideal situation. Those 20 MCQs were worth a possible 14% of his final mark and were too much to sacrifice when targeting the 55% or 65% pass mark. I know it may be difficult to follow my instructions, i.e. to allocate three hours and stick to it, but I believe that this practice is invaluable. What a waste of your study/revision effort to fail not because of a lack of knowledge, but because your timekeeping was at fault.

4. Answering correctly structured MCQs is one of the best methods of testing your knowledge.

5. The preparation involved in practising a full examination will assist in building your confidence to deal with the examination proper.

6. It will improve your exam technique by allowing you to see how easy it is to make a mistake, either by failing to read the question correctly or by reading too much into the question.

However you perform in the mock examination, I would strongly advise that you do not read too much into your result. Failing or passing this examination does not warrant despair or joy; this mock examination is primarily intended to give you practice and is not a predictor of performance in the examination proper.

I hope that your efforts are rewarded and wish you every success in your 2023 police promotion examination.

Paul Connor

Instructions for Completion

READ THE WHOLE OF THE INSTRUCTIONS BEFORE ATTEMPTING THE MOCK EXAMINATION

If you want to get the most from this mock examination, then you must treat it as if you were sitting the examination in paper form.

Time

You have up to three hours to complete the examination. It might not take you that long but it is best to assume that it will, so please make absolutely sure that you set aside three hours. You cannot expect to sit part of the examination for one hour, take a break for 20 minutes, return to the examination and then get an accurate picture of your performance. The examination must be completed in one three-hour sitting. However, if you have been allocated extra time to take the examination (for example, you may have been provided with reasonable adjustments because you are dyslexic), add that time to the standard three-hour examination time frame and if that includes breaks, take them—the idea is that the mock exam is taken in the same circumstances as you would take the examination proper.

Environment

You need to be able to concentrate on the examination and you cannot do that if the television is on, the phone is ringing etc. Find a place where you will not be disturbed for the duration of this examination and make sure that there are no distractions that will affect your performance.

Equipment

Ideally you will sit at a desk to take the mock examination. Trying to fill out the answer sheet on your lap whilst holding the question paper open will prove to be a difficult task to say the least. Make sure that you can see a clock, stopwatch or wristwatch.

You will need two pencils, a pencil sharpener and an eraser.

If you require any other materials in relation to reasonable adjustments, ensure they are available to you.

Pack 1

In Pack 1, you will find a blank answer sheet and the question booklet. Place both documents on the table.

When you decide to start the examination, please open the question booklet. Work through the test MCQs and make your choice of A, B, C or D by putting a horizontal line through the corresponding letter on the answer sheet.

Only mark one answer for each question.

Make sure that if you change your answer you erase the previous mark fully.

Try not to leave blank answers when you are unsure. Mark an answer and come back to the question if you have time at the end of the examination.

Pack 2

When you have finished the examination, open Pack 2 and begin the marking process. When you have finished marking your paper, please refer to the answer booklet for a detailed explanation of the correct answers with paragraph references to the *Blackstone's Police Manuals 2023*.

The marking process will take some time—to ensure accuracy, please do not rush this stage!

OXFORD
UNIVERSITY PRESS

Blackstone's Police Sergeants' and Inspectors' Mock Examination Paper 2023

Question Booklet

Time Allowed—180 minutes

1. Each of the questions is followed by four possible answers, only ONE of which is correct. Choose the ONE response that you consider to be correct. On the answer sheet mark the box that corresponds to your selection. Mark your answer clearly with a — mark. The answer sheet has spaces for your answers to all questions. If you change your mind about an answer, rub out the first mark, then mark your new answer. Mark only one answer for each question.

2. You are reminded that there is no need to read the whole examination paper before beginning to select answers to the questions posed.

3. You must ensure that BEFORE the close of the examination, all of your answers to the questions have been correctly entered on the answer sheet.

4. You may make any notes you wish on the question papers.

1. LAPORTE is unhappy about plans to build a prison near his home; he is particularly dissatisfied about the approach taken by Councillor MOSS who is supporting the planning application. LAPORTE knows MOSS lives in a house in a quiet residential street and stands outside MOSS's house at 09.00hrs holding a banner stating 'NO NEW PRISON HERE!' LAPORTE has a loudspeaker which he has turned up to full volume and is using to amplify his voice when he repeatedly shouts *'No new prison here!'* Several residents have complained about the noise and its impact, in particular the significant distress it is causing to them. PC ROWELL (on uniform patrol) attends the scene and speaks to LAPORTE who says that he has every right to protest in this manner.

Considering the powers to deal with protests under the Public Order Act 1986, which of the following comments is correct?

A PC ROWELL would have to call a supervisor to the scene (who must be an officer of the rank of inspector or above) to impose conditions on LAPORTE's protest.

B The Public Order Act 1986 does not provide powers to deal with 'one-person' protests and the officer would have to deal with the situation by using powers in other legislation.

C If PC ROWELL reasonably believes that the protest will result in serious public disorder or serious damage to property, then he may impose conditions on the protest.

D PC ROWELL may give directions imposing on LAPORTE such conditions as appear to be necessary to prevent the impact on local residents.

2. RANKINE is accused of committing an offence of theft from his employer. PC DAVISON arranges for RANKINE to voluntarily attend a police station to be interviewed regarding the offence. RANKINE attends the police station accompanied by FINLEY (RANKINE's legal representative). The interview takes place and RANKINE leaves having been told by PC DAVISON that he may be required to attend court in relation to the theft. It is decided that RANKINE should be charged with the theft and appear at magistrates' court to answer the charge.

In relation to the service of the written charge and requisition, which of the following comments is correct?

A They must be handed personally to RANKINE or posted to him at an address where it is reasonably believed that RANKINE will receive them (they could not be served on FINLEY).

B As RANKINE was legally represented, they must be served on FINLEY (they could not be served on RANKINE).

C These documents could be served by handing them in person to RANKINE or to FINLEY.

D The documents must be served physically (by handing them to RANKINE or FINLEY or being posted to an address where it is reasonably believed RANKINE or FINLEY will receive them); they cannot be served electronically.

3. GOLDMAN and CLARKE enter a bank. GOLDMAN approaches a cashier and hands over a note which states, '*Look right—near to the window*'. The cashier looks to his right and, on the other side of the bank, the cashier can see CLARKE (GOLDMAN's accomplice) holding a gun pointing towards the back of an old-age pensioner who is a customer at the bank. The old-age pensioner is completely unaware of the fact that CLARKE has a gun towards his back. GOLDMAN passes another note to the cashier which states, '*Hand over all the money or he gets shot!*' The cashier refuses. GOLDMAN speaks to CLARKE and says '*Do it!*' CLARKE strikes the back of the old-age pensioner's head with the butt of the gun. The customer falls to the ground and CLARKE points the gun at the customer. GOLDMAN looks at the cashier and states, '*Do you think I'm joking? Hand over the money or he gets shot!*' The cashier, fearing for the customer, hands over a large amount of cash.

At what point, if at all, has the offence of robbery been committed?

   A When GOLDMAN passes over the first note and the cashier can see the gun being pointed towards the back of the customer.
   B When GOLDMAN passes over the second note demanding the money.
   C When the cashier hands over a large amount of cash.
   D The offence of robbery has not been committed in these circumstances.

4. SAVILIA is lawfully arrested under s. 24A of the Police and Criminal Evidence Act 1984 by YORK (a civilian) for an offence of theft. PC HUTTON attends the scene of the arrest and takes SAVILIA into custody. Having considered the circumstances of the offence, PC HUTTON is satisfied that releasing SAVILIA on bail ('street bail') is necessary and proportionate.

Could SAVILIA be released on 'street bail' (s. 30A of the Police and Criminal Evidence Act 1984) in these circumstances?

   A No, because SAVILIA was arrested by YORK and not a police officer.
   B Yes, but an officer of the rank of inspector or above must authorise SAVILIA's release on bail.
   C No, as SAVILIA has been arrested for an indictable offence he must be taken to a designated police station.
   D Yes, although PC HUTTON could not attach conditions to any bail given to SAVILIA.

5. SANG has been charged with murder. SANG's defence team have disclosed details of a witness (ASPINALL) they propose to call as an alibi witness for the prosecution and the police officer in charge of the case, Inspector HERON, proposes to conduct an interview with ASPINALL.

In relation to the Code of Practice for Arranging and Conducting Interviews of Witnesses Notified by the Accused (under s. 21A of the Criminal Procedure and Investigations Act 1996), which of the following comments is correct?

   A ASPINALL is not entitled to be accompanied by a solicitor at the interview.
   B ASPINALL is not obliged to attend the proposed interview.
   C ASPINALL is entitled to be accompanied by a solicitor at the interview; the attendance of the solicitor will be funded by the Legal Services Commission.
   D ASPINALL must be interviewed by an officer of the rank of sergeant or above.

6. WALKER and BLEASEDALE are members of a gang who carry out offences of burglary. WALKER and BLEASEDALE along with the gang leader, CALLOW, are carrying out a burglary at a warehouse when they are disturbed by a security guard. CALLOW tells WALKER and BLEASEDALE to *'sort out'* the security guard by attacking him. The pair hesitate as they are not violent people. CALLOW says *'It's you two or him—kill him or I'll kill you both now!'* CALLOW has a violent past and so, believing they will be killed if they do not kill the security guard, they do as CALLOW demands. They attack the security guard and cause him life-threatening injuries—fortunately, the security guard survives. WALKER and BLEASEDALE are later arrested and charged with the attempted murder of the security guard (WALKER as a principal offender and BLEASEDALE as a secondary offender who aided the offence). Both state that they committed the offence under duress.

In relation to the defence of duress, which of the following comments is correct?

A The defence would not be available to either WALKER or BLEASEDALE as they are charged with attempted murder.

B The defence would be available to BLEASEDALE (as a secondary offender) but not to WALKER (the principal offender).

C The defence would be available to WALKER and BLEASEDALE as they were threatened with death if they did not commit the offence.

D The defence would not be available as WALKER and BLEASEDALE are part of a gang and the threat of death came from another gang member.

7. SHERRATT works in bar but his wages are not enough to support his lifestyle so he decides to commit offences of fraud and robbery to get extra cash. His plan is to serve customers at the bar and watch them. If they become drunk and then use credit or debit cards to pay for their drinks, he will 'clone' the card details and use the details to commit fraud offences. When they leave the bar, he will quickly follow them, attack them and steal from them. To commit the fraud offences, he brings a machine to clone the card details to his workplace; to commit the robbery offences he brings a balaclava and some pepper spray. He stores all of the items in a small storeroom next to the bar, intending to carry out the offences later that evening if the opportunity arises.

In relation to the offence of going equipped (contrary to s. 25 of the Theft Act 1968), which of the following comments is correct?

A SHERRATT does not commit the offence as robbery and fraud are not offences associated with the offence of going equipped.

B SHERRATT does not commit the offence as he does not have the items with him in a public place.

C SHERRATT commits the offence but only in respect of the balaclava and the pepper spray to be used in robbery offences.

D SHERRATT commits the offence but only in respect of the machine to clone the card details.

8. PC ANGUS is speaking to her supervisor, PS RYAN, about the Police (Conduct) Regulations 2020 and the Standards of Professional Behaviour. PC ANGUS asks PS RYAN what sanctions can be imposed on a police officer at a misconduct meeting if the conduct of the officer is found to amount to misconduct.

Which of the following would be a correct response?

A The lowest misconduct sanction available at a misconduct meeting is management advice.

B The sanctions imposed at a management meeting will be either a written warning or a final written warning.

C A sanction that could be imposed at a management meeting is a fine.

D The most severe sanction that could be imposed at a management meeting is a reduction in rank.

9. MARTINEZ (aged 16 years) is in custody at a designated police station after having been arrested for an offence of burglary (a recordable offence which is contrary to the Theft Act 1968). Non-intimate samples have not been obtained from MARTINEZ in the course of the investigation and DC GRAINGER, the officer in the case, now proposes to obtain those samples. MARTINEZ refuses to consent to the non-intimate samples being taken from him.

Which of the statements below is correct in relation to the taking of non-intimate samples in such a situation?

A As MARTINEZ is a juvenile, non-intimate samples cannot be obtained from him in this situation.

B An officer of the rank of inspector or above must authorise the taking of a non-intimate sample from MARTINEZ.

C A non-intimate sample cannot be taken from a detainee unless they provide written consent to the sample being taken.

D A non-intimate sample can be taken from MARTINEZ by force as long as a record is made of the circumstances and those present at the time the sample is obtained.

10. BOWDEN is 17 years old and is sitting in a park (a public place) next to OSMAN who is 19 years old. PC WATSON (on plain clothes foot patrol) walks past the pair and can see that BOWDEN is drinking from a can of lager. PC WATSON suspects BOWDEN is in possession of alcohol in a 'relevant place' so he identifies himself as a police officer and requires BOWDEN to surrender the can of lager using the power under s. 1 of the Confiscation of Alcohol (Young Persons) Act 1997 and also requires BOWDEN's name and address. OSMAN tells the officer to stop overreacting to the situation and explains that he gave BOWDEN the lager as it was a hot day and BOWDEN was thirsty. PC WATSON can see OSMAN has two cans of lager in a bag and suspects that he intends BOWDEN to drink them in the park. PC WATSON demands that OSMAN surrenders the two cans of lager and provides his name and address.

Has PC WATSON used his powers under s. 1 of the Confiscation of Alcohol (Young Persons) Act 1997 correctly?

A Yes, but only in relation to the surrender of the alcohol in BOWDEN's possession and requiring BOWDEN's name and address.

B No, as these powers are only available to an officer in uniform.

C Yes, he can require the surrender of the alcohol in the possession of BOWDEN and OSMAN and require their respective names and addresses.

D No, not unless an officer of the rank of inspector or above has authorised the use of the power and in doing so identified the 'relevant place' in which the power will be available and also the time frame that the power will be available from and to.

11. GREENOW has been arrested for an offence of fraud by PC LANG. The officer takes GREENOW to a designated police station and reports the facts of the arrest to the custody officer, PS FULAT. As soon as PC LANG finishes relating the circumstances of the arrest to PS FULAT, GREENOW says, *'It wasn't my idea—you know that someone else was involved, don't you?'*

Which of the following statements is correct with regard to the action that PS FULAT should take in response to this comment by GREENOW?

A PS FULAT may question GREENOW in respect of the comment he made in response to PC LANG's account.

B PS FULAT should note (on the custody record) any comment GREENOW makes in relation to PC LANG's account, but should not invite comment.

C PS FULAT need not make any note of the comment made by GREENOW.

D PS FULAT should caution GREENOW before asking any questions about the comment made in response to the circumstances of the arrest.

12. DODD is the owner of a breakfast/burger van which he pitches in a lay-by on a busy industrial estate. DODD is doing quite well as the quality of his food is good but his success is having an impact on LOWE's similar business which also operates from the industrial estate. LOWE has asked DODD to leave on several occasions and believes he has the right to do so as he was the first to do business on the estate; DODD has ignored him. LOWE is becoming desperate as his business is failing, so he hides an unloaded shotgun beneath his coat and visits DODD's van. DODD is not actually working in the van when LOWE arrives but WEIGHTMAN (DODD's girlfriend) is. LOWE tells WEIGHTMAN that DODD has one week to '*pack up and go*' or there will be consequences. When WEIGHTMAN asks what kind of consequences, LOWE reveals the shotgun and says, '*I will kill your boyfriend*'. LOWE has no intention of following through with his threat but does intend WEIGHTMAN to fear that he will kill DODD. In fact, WEIGHTMAN does not believe LOWE at all.

Considering only the offence of threats to kill (contrary to s. 16 of the Offences Against the Person Act 1861), which of the comments below is true?

A The offence is not committed by DODD as WEIGHTMAN does not believe the threat.
B DODD commits the offence in these circumstances.
C The offence is not committed as the threat was made to a third party (WEIGHTMAN).
D The threat must be made with the intention that the person who receives it will then and there fear for their life or the life of another. As the threat was made to kill DODD in a week's time, LOWE would not commit the offence.

13. UPTON approaches ALI (who does not know UPTON) and tells him that unless he kills PINTER immediately, his wife and child will be killed. UPTON produces a gun and several photographs of ALI's family and tells him that he has been observed for some time. UPTON gives ALI the gun and PINTER's details and, believing that UPTON will kill his wife and child, ALI goes to PINTER's house and kills him. ALI is arrested at the scene and states that the only reason he committed the offence was because he was placed under duress.

Would ALI be able to use this defence?

A No, as the defence is not available in respect of an offence of murder.
B Yes, as the threat drove ALI to commit the offence.
C No, as the threat of harm must be made solely to the person who goes on to commit the relevant offence.
D Yes, as the offence was carried out immediately after the threat was made.

14. DOOLEY breaks into a house owned by LOW with the intention of assaulting LOW and causing him injuries of a s. 47 (Offences Against the Person Act 1861) nature. He forces the front door of LOW's house and walks through the house into the lounge. Whilst in the lounge, he hears a noise upstairs and, believing it to be LOW, he grabs hold of a poker next to the fireplace in the lounge. DOOLEY does not intend to steal the poker but intends to use it on anyone who stands in his way. DOOLEY waits for a few minutes but nothing else happens. He is feeling a little nervous and decides he will keep the poker with him not only to protect himself but also to use it on LOW by smashing it into LOW's skull, thereby fracturing his skull and causing him grievous bodily harm (contrary to s. 18 of the Offences Against the Person Act 1861). DOOLEY moves from the lounge into the hallway of the house with that idea in his mind but then sees blue lights outside the front of the house and realises the police have arrived. He drops the poker in the hallway and runs out of the front door to escape.

Which of the following comments is correct in respect of the offence of burglary?

A DOOLEY commits a burglary (contrary to s. 9(1)(a) of the Theft Act 1968) when he enters the house to carry out a s. 47 assault on LOW.

B DOOLEY commits an aggravated burglary (contrary to s. 10 of the Theft Act 1968) when he picks up the poker.

C DOOLEY commits an aggravated burglary (contrary to s. 10 of the Theft Act 1968) when he enters the hallway of the house with the poker.

D DOOLEY does not commit an offence of burglary in these circumstances.

15. GLINSKI is planning to carry out a robbery at a post office and decides to use an air rifle during the offence as a means to threaten and frighten staff at the post office into doing as he demands. GLINSKI is convinced that the police are tracking his movements and wants to minimise the risk of his arrest and prosecution so he uses his 14-year-old nephew, PARRY, to take the air rifle to a garage at the rear of the post office and hide it next to several large bins. GLINSKI's plan is to make sure he is not followed to the post office and, once he is happy that that is the case, he will go to the bins, recover the air rifle and commit the robbery.

With regard to the offence of using someone to mind a weapon (contrary to s. 28(1) of the Violent Crime Reduction Act 2006), at what stage, if at all, has an offence first been committed by GLINSKI?

A No offence is committed by GLINSKI as the activity took place with an air weapon and this is not a 'dangerous weapon'.

B No offence is committed by GLINSKI as 'weapons' do not include firearms.

C The offence is first committed when GLINSKI uses PARRY to transport the air rifle to the rear of the post office.

D The offence is first committed when GLINSKI uses PARRY to hide the air rifle next to several large bins.

16. HAMPSON has been arrested on suspicion of rape and has been taken to a designated police station. HAMPSON is given his rights by the custody officer, PS CONWAY, and requests that he is represented by MOUAT (his solicitor) whilst he is in police custody. The officer in charge of the case, DC FRANCOMBE, believes that MOUAT will act in a way that will interfere with evidence connected to the rape.

    In relation to Code C and HAMPSON's right to legal advice, which of the following comments is correct?

    A DC FRANCOMBE should seek a superintendent's authority to deny HAMPSON access to legal advice from MOUAT.

    B HAMPSON should be allowed to speak with MOUAT but, to ensure that MOUAT acts ethically, his consultations with HAMPSON can be monitored by a police officer.

    C Once the decision has been taken to deny HAMPSON his legal advice, the authorisation applies to all solicitors or legal advisers and lasts up to a maximum of 36 hours.

    D HAMPSON cannot be denied access to legal advice from MOUAT in these circumstances.

17. PC FROBISHER is on uniform patrol when she is directed to a report of people riding pedal cycles in a dangerous way on a road outside a school. PC FROBISHER attends the scene and on arrival sees DRAY performing a 'wheelie' manoeuvre on a mountain bike on a road outside the school. PC FROBISHER approaches DRAY and requires him to stop, using her power under s. 163 of the Road Traffic Act 1988.

    Is the officer acting in a lawful manner when using the power under s. 163 of the Road Traffic Act 1988 to stop DRAY?

    A Yes, the power under s. 163 can be used to stop a mechanically propelled vehicle or a cycle on a road.

    B No, the power under s. 163 can only be used to stop a motor vehicle being driven on a road or public place.

    C Yes, the power under s. 163 can be used to stop a motor vehicle or a cycle on a road or public place.

    D No, the power under s. 163 can only be used to stop a mechanically propelled vehicle on a road.

18. GOWAN (who is 17 years old) is a witness to an offence of s. 18 wounding where the victim was stabbed with a knife. RUTHERFORD is arrested and charged with the offence and pleads 'not guilty' to it and a date has been set for the trial at Crown Court. GOWAN contacts the officer in the case, PC DEEN (who is also a witness in the case), and asks about the procedure in relation to her giving her witness evidence in the Crown Court.

Considering the law regarding special measures contained in the Youth Justice and Criminal Evidence Act 1999, which of the following comments is correct?

A Regardless of the nature of the offence, GOWAN is eligible to give evidence by video interview and the use of live link, but if she wishes to do so she can testify in the Crown Court.

B GOWAN is automatically eligible for a special measures direction; PC DEEN would not be eligible for a special measures direction.

C The primary rule is that all witnesses under the age of 18 must give their evidence via video interview and live link—a witness under the age of 18 is prohibited from testifying in Crown Court.

D GOWAN would be eligible for special measures only if she were in fear or distress about testifying.

19. GOUGH commits an offence under s. 4 of the Public Order Act 1986 (fear or provocation of violence). PC MAHROOF (an officer in uniform) visits GOUGH's home address to speak with GOUGH. When GOUGH answers the front door and sees the officer, he shouts *'Fuck off!'* and slams the door in the officer's face. PC MAHROOF reasonably believes that GOUGH is still on the premises and is considering his powers of entry to effect an arrest.

If PC MAHROOF considers it necessary to arrest GOUGH, could the officer enter and search the premises in order to arrest GOUGH using his powers of entry under s. 17 of the Police and Criminal Evidence Act 1984?

A Yes, but this is only because the officer is in uniform.

B No, as the offence under s. 4 of the Public Order Act 1986 is triable summarily only (it is not an indictable offence).

C Yes, and force may be used in exercising the power where it is necessary to do so.

D No, as GOUGH is not unlawfully at large and PC MAHROOF is not in 'hot pursuit' of him.

20. John AMBLER and Kate AMBLER are the parents of Jane AMBLER (who is 15 years old). John and Kate have separated resulting in a child arrangements order being made in respect of Jane AMBLER directing that she will live with her mother (Kate) at her home which is in Workington in Cumbria. Kate decides to take Jane on a holiday visiting Scotland and then flying to Norway—the holiday lasts three weeks. John AMBLER only discovers that Kate has taken Jane on the holiday after she returns from Norway and he complains to the police that this is an offence of child abduction by Kate AMBLER.

Would Kate AMBLER have committed an offence of child abduction (contrary to s. 1 of the Child Abduction Act 1984) in these circumstances?

A No, as the offence relates to a child under the age of 14 (and Jane is 15 years old).

B Yes, the offence is complete when Kate takes Jane to Scotland.

C No, Kate is named in a child arrangements order as a person with whom Jane will live and she has taken her out of the United Kingdom for a period of less than one month.

D Yes, the offence is complete when Kate takes Jane to Norway.

21. BERRY is fascinated by Adolf Hitler and the Nazi Party and their treatment and extermination of millions of people in concentration camps in the 1930s and 1940s. He has a collection of Nazi memorabilia on display in the rear living room of his house, including a large swastika flag which has 'Tod der Juden!' ('Death to Jews!') written on it. KAPLAN (who is a Jew) sees the flag and words written on it when he is standing in the rear bedroom of a house that backs on to BERRY's house. KAPLAN is extremely upset at what he sees and contacts the police.

Has BERRY committed an offence under s. 29B of the Public Order Act 1986 (use of words or behaviour or display of written material)?

A Yes, although BERRY would have a defence if he believed the flag on display could not be seen by a person outside his dwelling.

B No, as the written material is displayed by a person inside a dwelling and not seen except by other persons in that or another dwelling.

C Yes, as the flag is threatening and can be seen from outside BERRY's dwelling.

D No, not unless BERRY intends to stir up religious hatred.

22. Using her powers under s. 1 of the Police and Criminal Evidence Act 1984, PC KAY (who is on uniform foot patrol) stops and searches a Ford Focus motor vehicle which is being driven by JOLIE; JOLIE is the only person in the vehicle. PC KAY searches JOLIE and the vehicle for the same object and using the same grounds (searching for stolen property) but does not find anything. Enquiries in relation to the vehicle reveal that CHAMBERS is the owner of the vehicle. PC KAY makes a written record of the search on the spot using a single search record to record the search of JOLIE and the vehicle. She provides a copy of the record to JOLIE.

Has PC KAY complied with the requirements created by the Police and Criminal Evidence Act 1984 and Code A of the Codes of Practice?

   A Yes, and as a search record was provided to JOLIE (the person in charge of the vehicle), CHAMBERS would have no entitlement to a copy of the search record.
   B No, a separate record should have been made for each search (the search of JOLIE and the search of the vehicle).
   C Yes, but if CHAMBERS asks for a copy of the record of search then he is entitled to one if he makes the request within three months beginning on the date the vehicle was searched.
   D No, where the owner of the vehicle searched is not present, the officer carrying out the search should leave a notice in the vehicle stating that it has been searched.

23. Authority has been given for TOMPKINS (a 20-year-old who has been arrested and is in police detention for an offence of possession with intention to supply a Class A drug) to be subject to an intimate search (under s. 55(1) of the Police and Criminal Evidence Act 1984). The search will be to recover a Class A drug that TOMPKINS is believed to have concealed in his rectum.

Which of the following comments is correct in relation to the person who can carry out that search and the location of the search?

   A The search can be carried out by a police officer at a police station.
   B An intimate search of this type can only take place at a hospital.
   C An intimate search of this type may take place at a surgery.
   D The search can be carried out by a police officer at a hospital.

24. NEWMAN (a resident of the United Kingdom) goes on a business trip to Turkey. During his trip, he is in a restaurant when he overhears a conversation between two men who are talking about planting a bomb at Heathrow Airport in a month's time. The men state that the bomb will kill hundreds of people and that when it explodes they will claim it as a victory for al-Qaeda against the British government. NEWMAN believes that the information he has heard could help to prevent an act of terrorism. NEWMAN flies home to England two days later but does not say anything to anyone about the conversation he overheard in Turkey.

With regard to the offence of information about acts of terrorism (contrary to s. 38B of the Terrorism Act 2000), which of the following comments is correct?

A NEWMAN must disclose the information as soon as reasonably practicable and this disclosure can be made to any person in authority.

B NEWMAN would commit this offence as he believes the information he has might be of material assistance in preventing an act of terrorism.

C As NEWMAN was outside the country when he became aware of the information, he could not be charged with this offence if he failed to disclose that information.

D NEWMAN has committed this offence to which there is no defence.

25. DORMLEY is a supervisor of a team of 20 office employees. He becomes involved in a confrontation with another member of staff, resulting in DORMLEY punching the other member of staff in the back of the head—this is reported to the police and an investigation into the offence commences. ESTERTON witnessed the incident and DORMLEY believes ESTERTON is a potential witness in any proceedings against him for the offence. DORMLEY is concerned about possible criminal charges and approaches ESTERTON. Intending to intimidate ESTERTON, he tells ESTERTON that if he says anything about what he has seen then he will get a terrible staff report and miss his wages bonus. ESTERTON tells DORMLEY that he is not interested and if the police ask him, he will tell them what he saw. DORMLEY takes a different approach and tells ESTERTON not to say anything otherwise he will be assaulted; ESTERTON is sure he can deal with DORMLEY and is not intimidated at all.

Does DORMLEY commit the offence of intimidating witnesses and jurors (contrary to s. 51 of the Criminal Justice and Public Order Act 1994)?

A No, as ESTERTON is not actually a witness or a juror.

B Yes, the offence is committed when DORMLEY tells ESTERTON that he will get a poor staff report which will affect his wages.

C No, as ESTERTON is not intimidated by the actions of DORMLEY.

D Yes, the offence is committed but only when DORMLEY threatens ESTERTON with violence.

26. WEIR is employed by his local council as a maintenance manager. He has responsibility for a number of council employees who visit council houses and carry out maintenance and repairs to the premises. WEIR tells several of his workers to visit a council house occupied by FRATTEN and carry out extensive refurbishment there. The house is not owned by the council, it is FRATTEN's private property and FRATTEN is WEIR's girlfriend. One of the council workers is suspicious about the job and, after the work has been carried out, he reports the matter to the police by speaking to PC JAMES. PC JAMES notes down some basic details on a piece of paper and tells the council worker that he will look into the matter. PC JAMES places the paper in his coat pocket and fully intends to investigate the matter but because he is so busy at work he accidentally forgets about the incident and no investigation takes place.

Considering the offence of misconduct in a public office (contrary to common law), which of the following statements is true?

A The offence has not been committed as WEIR is not a police officer and PC JAMES's lack of action was purely accidental.

B PC JAMES has committed the offence (his omission makes him liable) but WEIR has not committed the offence.

C WEIR and PC JAMES have committed the offence in these circumstances.

D Only WEIR has committed the offence in these circumstances.

27. LESTER is in a pub drinking with several friends. THATCHER storms into the pub and approaches LESTER and accuses him of having an affair with his wife (LESTER is a friend of THATCHER's wife but is not having an affair with her). THATCHER shouts that if LESTER does not stop the affair he will tell LESTER's wife and children about the affair and wreck LESTER's life. LESTER tells THATCHER that he is imagining things and that there is no affair taking place. THATCHER shouts *'Right—if you won't admit it, I'll mess your life up and tell your wife and kids now!'* LESTER feels seriously wronged by the accusation and the threat to his family life and loses his temper with THATCHER; he attacks him intending to kill him. Although THATCHER is very badly injured, he survives the attack and LESTER is charged with attempted murder. LESTER states that he lost control when THATCHER threatened to tell his wife and children about a non-existent affair.

Could LESTER use the 'special defence' of loss of control in these circumstances?

A No, as the thing said that caused him to lose control (the 'qualifying trigger') was connected to an accusation of sexual infidelity.

B No, as the loss of control was not related to a fear of serious violence from THATCHER.

C No, as he lost control in relation to a thing threatened to be done rather than a thing done.

D No, as the charge he faces is one of attempted murder and not murder.

28. PC WHITLEY (an officer with five years' police service) has attended a first stage meeting regarding her unsatisfactory performance. Her supervisor, PS KEARNEY (PC WHITLEY's line manager), has listened to PC WHITLEY's representations in the meeting but considers that PC WHITLEY's performance is unsatisfactory. Consequently, a written improvement notice is sent to PC WHITLEY setting out the relevant performance issue and the improvement required. The notice also includes the relevant 'specified period' within which improvement is expected to be made.

Which one of the following comments is correct in relation to that 'specified period'?

A It is expected that the specified period for improvement would not normally exceed one month.

B A specified period set out after a first stage meeting can only be extended at a second stage meeting.

C It is expected that the specified period for improvement would not normally exceed three months.

D If a specified period is extended, the extension should not lead to the improvement period exceeding six months.

29. FEATHERSTONE visits a country show with his family and parks his car on a makeshift car park situated within the grounds of the private estate where the country show is taking place. FEATHERSTONE returns to his car several hours later and finds that his car has been blocked in by another car owned by JACKSON. FEATHERSTONE waits for 30 minutes but there is no sign of JACKSON, so FEATHERSTONE opens the door of JACKSON's car, releases the handbrake and, standing outside the car, he pushes it 15 feet so that it no longer causes an obstruction. FEATHERSTONE believes that he has the lawful authority to do so as JACKSON's car was blocking his exit.

Would this constitute an offence of taking a conveyance (contrary to s. 12 of the Theft Act 1968)?

A No, the offence has not been committed as the activity took place on private land not a road or other public place.

B Yes, the offence has been committed but FEATHERSTONE would have a defence as he believed that he had lawful authority to take the conveyance.

C No, the offence has not been committed as JACKSON's car has not been used as a conveyance.

D Yes, the offence has been committed and FEATHERSTONE would have no defence of 'lawful authority' as he is not a police officer, council worker or agent of a finance company repossessing a vehicle.

30. PC BUNN is on uniform patrol and is sent to a report of children drinking alcohol in a public park. When the officer arrives in the park, she can see EVERITT (aged 15 years) and LEWIS (aged 16 years) sitting on a park bench drinking from cans labelled as cider. PC BUNN speaks to EVERITT and LEWIS, establishes their ages and that they are drinking alcohol (the cans of cider). EVERITT has an unopened can of cider with her as well as the opened one she is drinking from. PC BUNN requires EVERITT and LEWIS to surrender the opened cans of cider and EVERITT to surrender the unopened can of cider. PC BUNN pours the cider from all of the cans down a drain and throws the empty cans in a bin.

In relation to the powers provided by s. 1 of the Confiscation of Alcohol (Young Persons) Act 1997, which of the following comments is correct?

A PC BUNN can remove EVERITT and LEWIS to their place of residence.
B The officer did not have a power to require the surrender of the unopened can of cider from EVERITT.
C PC BUNN can remove EVERITT to a place of safety and, if necessary, this could be a police station.
D The officer did not have the power to pour the cider down a drain.

31. Due to significant and continuing problems with children and young people truanting from school and being involved in anti-social behaviour, a local authority has decided to authorise the powers available under s. 16 of the Crime and Disorder Act 1998 and has 'designated premises' within its area as a place to which children and young people of compulsory school age may be removed to.

In relation to the law under s. 16 of the Act (dealing with the removal of truants and excluded pupils to designated premises), which of the following comments is correct?

A The police officer directing that the powers available under the Act shall be available will be an officer of the rank of superintendent or above.
B A constable must have reasonable cause to suspect that a child is a truant or is an excluded pupil in order to use the powers that the Act provides.
C A constable using the power to remove a child or young person to 'designated premises' must be in uniform.
D The power is available if the child or young person is found in a private or public place.

32. John and Bridget EDMONSON (both 39 years old) are married and live in a house together with Bridget EDMONSON's 60-year-old mother COLOHAN. The relationship between John and Bridget EDMONSON has deteriorated, resulting in John EDMONSON threatening violence towards Bridget EDMONSON on several occasions. COLOHAN has witnessed the threats being made and contacts the police who attend the house during an argument between John and Bridget EDMONSON; the police witness John EDMONSON threatening violence towards Bridget EDMONSON. As a result, the police consider that issuing a domestic violence protection notice (a DVPN) under s. 24 of the Crime and Security Act 2010 is necessary to protect Bridget EDMONSON.

In relation to the issuing of such a DVPN, which of the following comments is correct?

A If Bridget EDMONSON does not consent to the issuing of a DVPN, then a DVPN cannot be issued.

B The officer authorising the DVPN must consider any representations made by John EDMONSON as to the issuing of a DVPN.

C If a DVPN is issued, then the authorising officer must apply to a magistrates' court for a Domestic Violence Protection Order (a DVPO) no later than 24 hours after the DVPN was issued.

D A DVPN could not require John EDMONSON to leave the house he lives in with Bridget EDMONSON.

33. COMB (a 17-year-old male) approaches NEWTON (a 15-year-old female) in a park and the two chat for 30 minutes, during which time NEWTON tells COMB her age. COMB asks NEWTON if she will meet him at the same location the following day for another chat; NEWTON agrees. The following morning, COMB decides that he will try to touch NEWTON's genitals if he can and walks to the park with that intention; however, he waits at the park in vain as NEWTON has decided not to bother meeting him.

Considering the offence of meeting a child following sexual grooming (contrary to s. 15 of the Sexual Offences Act 2003), which of the following comments is correct?

A The offence is committed when COMB walks to the park as he is travelling to meet NEWTON with the intention of carrying out an offence of sexual activity with a child (contrary to s. 9 of the Sexual Offences Act 2003).

B The offence has not been committed because the communications between the two were not of a sexual nature.

C The offence has not been committed as NEWTON did not meet COMB in the park (on a second occasion).

D The offence has not been committed because COMB is under 18.

34. DC FAYED is working in the Criminal Investigation Department at his station when he receives good-quality intelligence from a trusted source in relation to the location of a large amount of stolen goods. The stolen property is alleged to be located at five different premises and, after briefly discussing the matter with his supervisor, DC FAYED decides to make an application to search all the premises (an 'all premises' warrant). Due to the nature of the intelligence received by DC FAYED, he decides to request that the warrant allow entry to the target premises on multiple occasions.

In relation to the procedures under ss. 15 and 16 of the Police and Criminal Evidence Act 1984 (application for a warrant and execution of a warrant) and Code B of the Codes of Practice, which of the following comments is correct?

   A Applications for multiple premises and multiple entry warrants must be made with the written authority of an officer of at least the rank of superintendent (although in urgent cases where a superintendent is not readily available, the most senior officer on duty may authorise the application).

   B Entry and search under such a warrant must be made within one month from the date of its issue.

   C No premises may be entered or searched for the second or any subsequent time under a warrant which authorises multiple entries unless a police officer of at least the rank of inspector has, in writing, authorised that entry to those premises.

   D If the warrant is an all premises warrant, no premises which are not specified in it may be entered and searched unless a police officer of at least the rank of superintendent has, in writing, authorised them to be entered.

35. LORIMER is a Police Community Support Officer visiting a newsagents owned by GRACE who has complained about anti-social behaviour in the area. LORIMER is chatting to GRACE in the shop when she sees YORK acting in a very odd way in the shop. LORIMER forms the suspicion that YORK is committing an offence of theft and decides to arrest YORK using the power of arrest available under s. 24A of the Police and Criminal Evidence Act 1984. When LORIMER is later asked why she arrested YORK, she states that it was not reasonably practicable for a constable to make the arrest instead of her and she had reasonable grounds to believe that YORK would make off before a constable could assume responsibility for him.

Considering the power of arrest under s. 24A of the Police and Criminal Evidence Act 1984, which of the following comments is correct?

   A LORIMER should not have arrested YORK as the power of arrest under s. 24A is not available to a Police Community Support Officer.

   B In this situation, LORIMER has acted correctly and this is a lawful arrest.

   C As theft is triable either way, this is an unlawful arrest (the power can only be exercised in relation to an indictable offence).

   D This is an unlawful arrest as the power can only be used where the person reasonably believes (not suspects) that a person is committing an indictable offence.

36. A private members' club holds a 'stag' evening in a building the club owns. The intention is to have a dinner which will be followed by several female lap dancer acts—those attending have been promised by the organiser that the lap dancers will engage in sexual acts with men attending the event. Thirty men attend the event and during the evening they drink a large amount of alcohol meaning that they are all extremely drunk when HOPKINSON, the first lap dancer, takes the stage. Because of the conduct of the men, HOPKINSON runs off the stage and hides behind the bar. The group become agitated and all threaten violence towards HOPKINSON, demanding that she return to the stage and perform a sex act. TAWLEY, SMITH and OWEN are particularly nasty as they run behind the bar and physically drag HOPKINSON back to the stage, punching her several times in the process.

Has an offence of riot (contrary to s. 1 of the Public Order Act 1986) been committed in this situation?

A No, as riot cannot be committed in a private place—it can only be committed in public.
B Yes, but only TAWLEY, SMITH and OWEN are guilty of the offence.
C No, as only three persons used violence rather than 12 or more.
D Yes, all the men at the event commit the offence.

37. NORRIS is an electrician and visits a Catholic church to carry out some minor repairs on a faulty switch. As NORRIS walks out of the church, LEWIN sees him and presumes NORRIS to be a Catholic. LEWIN intensely dislikes Catholics and decides to damage NORRIS's property because of his hostility towards them. He follows NORRIS to his van and, as NORRIS is opening the van door, LEWIN kicks the van door causing criminal damage to it (contrary to s. 1(1) of the Criminal Damage Act 1971). In fact, NORRIS is a Protestant.

Based on these circumstances alone, has LEWIN committed a religiously aggravated offence?

A Yes, the offence is motivated by religious hostility.
B No, as NORRIS is not a Catholic.
C Yes, all offences under the Criminal Damage Act 1971 can be racially and/or religiously aggravated.
D No, there has been no demonstration of hostility from LEWIN.

38. PC BAINES is on uniform patrol when he is approached by DONEGAN who tells the officer that he has just seen MATTHEWS driving a car at speed along a nearby road. DONEGAN states that he heard a loud bang as MATTHEWS drove along the road and thinks that MATTHEWS has struck a parked car. PC BAINES believes that an accident has taken place and several minutes later PC BAINES stops the car driven by MATTHEWS.

In relation to procedures following an accident (under s. 6(5) of the Road Traffic Act 1988), can PC BAINES require MATTHEWS to take a preliminary breath test?

A No, because an accident must have actually taken place. PC BAINES's belief that an accident has taken place is not enough to meet the requirement.

B Yes, but the preliminary breath test can only take place at or near the place where the requirement to cooperate with the test is imposed.

C No, as PC BAINES must believe or suspect that MATTHEWS has been drinking.

D Yes, but only if PC BAINES reasonably believes that MATTHEWS has failed to stop at the scene of an accident.

39. FLACK had a short relationship with STIRLING but STIRLING broke up with FLACK. FLACK wants revenge against STIRLING and wishes to cause him problems but is scared of doing anything herself so she encourages BEST to cause criminal damage to a VW Golf car owned by STIRLING. BEST agrees and visits STIRLING's house. He sees a VW Golf outside STIRLING's house and slashes all the tyres with a knife but he has made a mistake as the car does not belong to STIRLING—it belongs to DUTTON. DUTTON sees BEST damaging his car and confronts BEST. In the struggle that follows, BEST commits a s. 39 battery offence (contrary to the Criminal Justice Act 1988) against DUTTON.

In relation to the criminal damage and the battery, would the doctrine of transferred *mens rea* apply to FLACK in these circumstances?

A Yes, but FLACK would only be liable as an accessory to the criminal damage to DUTTON's car.

B No, the doctrine has no applicability in this situation as it is only relevant when considering offences against the person under the Offences Against the Person Act 1861.

C Yes, FLACK is liable as an accessory to the criminal damage and s. 39 battery offence.

D No, transferred *mens rea* does not apply to FLACK as he is an accessory—the doctrine only has applicability when considering the actions of a principal offender.

40. FORBES and her boyfriend, PRICE, are having a loud and prolonged dispute inside their home. The noise has disturbed several of their neighbours who have contacted the police. PC VESEY attends the scene and is let into the house by FORBES and led into the lounge where PRICE is. In front of PRICE, FORBES tells the officer that she has discovered PRICE has been sleeping with other women and that she wants him out of her house (the house belongs to FORBES). PRICE responds by saying to FORBES, *'As soon as this copper has gone, I will smash everything of yours in this house!'*

With regard to the law relating to a breach of the peace, which of the following comments is true?

A PC VESEY cannot arrest PRICE for a breach of the peace because the threat to FORBES's property was made in private (FORBES's house).

B PC VESEY cannot arrest PRICE for breach of the peace because the threat was to harm a person's property and not to harm a person.

C PC VESEY can arrest PRICE for a breach of the peace and he could be detained at a police station until there is no further likelihood of a reoccurrence of the breach of the peace.

D PC VESEY can arrest PRICE for a breach of the peace and once he has been taken to a police station, he could be bailed to appear at court in relation to the charge.

41. PURCELL is suspected of carrying out a minor assault on BROWN. PC GREALEY is investigating the case and asks PURCELL to attend a police station to be interviewed regarding the assault. PC GREALEY does not arrest PURCELL who, although told of all his rights, states that he does not need or want any legal advice. During the interview PC GREALEY notices a medium-sized tear in the fabric of a coat that PURCELL is wearing and believes that this may be attributable to PURCELL's participation in the assault. PC GREALEY asks PURCELL to account for the tear and PURCELL states that he did it when he was leaving his house that morning by catching it on a door frame. PC GREALEY does not believe PURCELL.

Could PC GREALEY give PURCELL a 'special warning' (under s. 36 of the Criminal Justice and Public Order Act 1994) in relation to the damage to his coat?

A Yes, as PC GREALEY does not believe the account that PURCELL gives in relation to the damage to his coat.

B No, as PURCELL has not been arrested.

C Yes, although the 'special warning' must be given to PURCELL immediately after his response to the question(s) regarding the damage to his coat.

D No, as PURCELL does not have a solicitor with him in the interview.

42. SHIPP and CHALLICE work on the same shift in a jewellery shop owned by AKERS. One afternoon, SHIPP sees CHALLICE behaving in a suspicious manner by fumbling around in her handbag and seemingly placing something in it that looks like a gold bangle. SHIPP suspects that CHALLICE has stolen an item of jewellery from the shop but is not sure. Several days later, PC EAGLE attends the jewellery shop and speaks to members of staff as AKERS has notified the police of a series of thefts from the shop. PC EAGLE speaks to the staff as a group and asks them if they have seen anything suspicious while working in the shop. SHIPP remembers CHALLICE's behaviour but remains silent when the question is posed to the group as he does not like the police and knows that CHALLICE is having some financial problems. PC EAGLE later speaks to the staff individually and asks SHIPP if he knows anything about the thefts—SHIPP replies that he has seen nothing that would help the police.

Does SHIPP commit an offence of assisting an offender (contrary to s. 4 of the Criminal Law Act 1967)?

A Yes, the offence is committed by SHIPP when he remains silent in response to the initial question posed to the group by PC EAGLE.

B No, the offence has not been committed by SHIPP as he is only suspicious that CHALLICE is guilty of theft from the shop.

C Yes, but only when he lies to the officer in response to a direct question when spoken to as an individual.

D No, as an offence of theft is not a 'relevant offence'.

43. COGAN (aged 17 years) is on holiday and sitting on a bench on a seafront smoking cannabis. PC TOOMER is walking behind the bench; he smells the cannabis and sees COGAN smoking. PC TOOMER approaches COGAN and lawfully searches him under s. 23 of the Misuse of Drugs Act 1971. During the search, PC TOOMER finds a small amount of cannabis in COGAN's pocket and, as the officer finds the drug, COGAN says, *'It's only a little bit—just for me on holiday'*. PC TOOMER is satisfied that the cannabis he has found is only for personal use by COGAN.

Could PC TOOMER deal with COGAN by way of a Penalty Notice for Disorder (PND) in respect of possession of the cannabis?

A No, as cannabis is a Class B drug and the scheme only relates to Class C drugs.

B Yes, such a PND could be issued to anyone who is 16 or over.

C No, PNDs are not appropriate for offenders under the age of 18.

D Yes, a PND can be used for possession of any drug as long as the drug is possessed for personal use.

44. WAYMAN split up from LIGHTFOOT (her long-standing boyfriend). The split was acrimonious and WAYMAN has heard that since the break-up LIGHTFOOT has started a new relationship with BAILEY. WAYMAN possesses a number of pictures of her and LIGHTFOOT having sexual intercourse and, in order to cause distress to BAILEY, WAYMAN sends the pictures to BAILEY by post. BAILEY receives the pictures but actually finds them amusing and is not at all upset by seeing them.

Has WAYMAN committed an offence of disclosing private sexual photographs and films with intent to cause distress (contrary to s. 3 of the Criminal Justice and Courts Act 2015)?

A Yes, as WAYMAN intends to cause BAILEY distress.

B No, as the pictures were not delivered by an electronic medium.

C Yes, as the pictures were likely to cause distress to anyone who saw them.

D No, as WAYMAN's intention was to cause BAILEY distress rather than LIGHTFOOT.

45. PC DUNBAR is a serving police officer working for Police Scotland and is on holiday in Kendal (in Cumbria, England) when he sees MILLER walking through Kendal. MILLER is wanted on suspicion of committing a large number of burglaries in the Dumfries and Galloway district of Police Scotland. If MILLER were in Scotland, it would be lawful for PC DUNBAR to arrest him.

Can PC DUNBAR arrest MILLER in England for the burglary offences that occurred in Scotland?

A No, an officer from Police Scotland may not arrest a person in England or Wales unless they are accompanied by a police constable from an English or Welsh police force.

B Yes, and after arrest PC DUNBAR must take MILLER to the nearest police station in the police area he has been arrested in.

C No, an officer from Police Scotland may not arrest a person in England or Wales.

D Yes, and after arrest PC DUNBAR must take MILLER to a designated police station in Scotland or the nearest designated police station in England.

46. PC CROSSFIELD attends the scene of a theft of cash from an office block. When the officer walks into the office, she is approached by LINTON who states, '*Officer, I stole the money. I want to confess.*' LINTON is arrested for theft and taken to a designated police station. PC CROSSFIELD records the comment made by LINTON as soon as practicable, noting when it was made and signing it in her pocket book.

Which of the following comments is correct regarding the comment made by LINTON to PC CROSSFIELD?

A It is a 'significant statement' and it should be put to LINTON at the beginning of the interview with him, after caution and before questioning.

B It is not a 'significant statement' as it was made at an office block rather than at a designated police station.

C It is a 'significant statement' and it should be put to LINTON at the conclusion of any interview with him and at the end of questioning.

D It is not a 'significant statement' as it was not made in response to and after any form of caution.

47. BRUSHETT has been arrested on suspicion of committing an offence under s. 30 of the Sexual Offences Act 2003 (sexual activity with a person with a mental disorder impeding choice); the touching involved penetration of the victim by BRUSHETT. BRUSHETT has been interviewed and charged with the offence and the issue of bail is being considered. The custody officer, PS WINTER, is aware that BRUSHETT has a single previous conviction which was for an offence of assault by penetration (contrary to s. 2 of the Sexual Offences Act 2003).

Would the provisions of s. 25 of the Criminal Justice and Public Order Act 1994 (police bail restrictions) be applicable to BRUSHETT?

A No, BRUSHETT does not have a conviction for an offence under s. 30 of the Sexual Offences Act 2003.

B Yes, and bail shall be granted if PS WINTER is of the opinion that there are exceptional circumstances which justify it.

C No, BRUSHETT has not been charged with an offence of murder, attempted murder or manslaughter.

D Yes, and as a consequence BRUSHETT cannot be granted bail in any circumstances.

48. CROFTON knocks on the door of a house owned by WOODWARD. CROFTON tells WOODWARD that he was walking past WOODWARD's house and noticed that the roof was in need of emergency repairs. CROFTON tells WOODWARD that it will not cost much (only £150) and he is in a position to do the work immediately but only if WOODWARD pays him £150 there and then. WOODWARD gives CROFTON £150 and CROFTON promises WOODWARD that he will start the work immediately and states that he will go and get his tools and the equipment to carry out the repairs as he has these in his van which he has parked nearby. CROFTON walks off and does not return; the truth of the matter is that CROFTON never intended to carry out the work.

In relation to the offence of fraud by false representation (contrary to s. 2 of the Fraud Act 2006), which of the following comments is correct?

A The offence has not been committed as the representation that is false must be one as to fact or law—this is a broken promise.

B The offence has been committed as CROFTON's statement (that he will repair the roof) is false—it misrepresents his actual intentions as he never intended to keep the promise he made.

C The offence has been committed although it will be tried summarily as this is low-value fraud (the value of the goods fraudulently obtained does not exceed £200).

D The offence has been committed but would only be complete when WOODWARD gave CROFTON the £150.

49. PCs WARD and HUGHES (both male officers) are on uniform mobile patrol when they are directed to an address where two men have been seen acting suspiciously in the garden of a dwelling house. When the officers arrive at the address, they see MARTIN standing in the front garden of the dwelling house and standing inside the hallway of the dwelling house they see VICKERY. The officers reasonably suspect that MARTIN and VICKERY may have stolen articles on their person and wish to use their powers under s. 1 of the Police and Criminal Evidence Act 1984 to search both men.

Thinking about the issues in respect of s. 1 of the Police and Criminal Evidence Act 1984 and Code A of the Codes of Practice, can the officers search MARTIN and/or VICKERY?

A Yes, if they reasonably believe MARTIN does not reside in the dwelling and is there without the express or implied permission of someone who resides in the dwelling; they cannot search VICKERY.

B No, as search powers under s. 1 of the Police and Criminal Evidence Act 1984 cannot be exercised in a garden used as part of a dwelling or in any dwelling house.

C Yes, they could search both men if they reasonably suspect that they do not live in the dwelling house.

D No, not unless the officers reasonably believe that MARTIN and VICKERY do not reside in the dwelling and that they are in the dwelling or on land used with it without the permission of the owner of the premises.

50. DELANEY is in police detention having been arrested for an offence of assault by penetration (contrary to s. 2 of the Sexual Offences Act 2003). A witness statement from the victim of the offence has been obtained which includes a description of the person responsible for the attack. The victim states that her attacker had a large scar on his left hip and the officer in the case, DC BUTCHER, is considering whether DELANEY could be examined to establish if he has such a scar (using the powers under s. 54A(1) of the Police and Criminal Evidence Act 1984).

In relation to such an examination, which of the comments below is correct?

A DELANEY cannot be examined to establish if he has a scar on his hip as the purpose of s. 54A(1) is solely to establish the identity of the person concerned.

B DELANEY can be examined to discover if he has the scar on his hip but such an examination cannot be carried out using force.

C If DELANEY refuses, then an officer of the rank of inspector or above can orally authorise that DELANEY be examined to establish if he has the scar on his hip.

D An inspector must give an authorisation for DELANEY's hip to be examined regardless of whether DELANEY provides his consent to the examination.

51. ARCHER is seven months pregnant and becomes involved in an argument with TREVINO. Intending to cause ARCHER serious harm, TREVINO produces a knife and stabs ARCHER in the stomach. This causes serious injury to ARCHER and also injures ARCHER's unborn child. ARCHER is rushed to hospital where she prematurely gives birth to her child which lives for two days but then dies as a direct consequence of the injuries it received as an unborn child when TREVINO stabbed ARCHER. ARCHER makes a full recovery from her injuries.

Is TREVINO liable for the death of the child?

   A No, as TREVINO did not intend to kill ARCHER.
   B Yes, TREVINO would be liable for the manslaughter of the child.
   C No, as the doctrine of transferred *mens rea* does not apply in a case such as this.
   D Yes, TREVINO would be liable for the murder of the child.

52. KIRBY owns a field and has called the police because he is having problems with trespassers. HYDE, O'KANE and RYAN drove onto the land in a 4 × 4 vehicle towing a caravan and have been camped on the site for two days. When KIRBY discovered their presence, he told them to leave. In response, all three shouted abusive words to KIRBY and HYDE told KIRBY to '*Fuck off or I'll kick your head in.*'

Could a direction to leave the land under s. 61 of the Criminal Justice and Public Order Act 1994 be given to HYDE, O'KANE and RYAN?

   A Yes, but only to HYDE as he was the only person to threaten the occupier (KIRBY) with violence.
   B No, they do not have six or more vehicles between them.
   C Yes, as they have used threatening, abusive or insulting words or behaviour towards the occupier (KIRBY) of the land.
   D No, the direction can only be given to a group of five or more people trespassing on land with the common purpose of residing on the land.

53. NOONAN has committed an offence of fraud and a warrant for his arrest has been issued by a justice of the peace. PC OMAR is trying to locate NOONAN to execute the warrant but is having difficulty doing so. PC OMAR believes that NOONAN's ex-employer (a local authority) has information which would enable the officer to track NOONAN down and execute the warrant. It is suggested that a disclosure order could be obtained (under s. 125CA of the Magistrates' Courts Act 1980) to require the local authority to supply information about NOONAN.

If such an order is made, what information about NOONAN could be required from the local authority?

A His name, date of birth or national insurance number and his address (or any of his addresses).

B His address (or any of his addresses) and any vehicle details that may assist in establishing his location.

C Any financial details (bank accounts and credit arrangements) that could lead to establishing his whereabouts.

D Any driving licence or passport details that could assist in tracing him for the purpose of executing the warrant of arrest.

54. MANNIGER is sick to death of the behaviour of SMITH who is in the habit of parking his car outside MANNIGER's house and playing his music extremely loudly and late at night causing MANNIGER to lose sleep. One evening, MANNIGER has had enough and goes out to the street and confronts SMITH who is sitting in the driving seat of his car with his girlfriend, INCE, sitting in the front passenger seat. MANNIGER states, *'If you don't stop playing that loud music, I'll follow you home and pour paint stripper all over this car!'* MANNIGER intends SMITH to fear that his car will be damaged. SMITH is completely unconcerned by the threat and does not believe MANNIGER although INCE does believe the threat.

With regard to the offence of threats to destroy or damage property (contrary to s. 2 of the Criminal Damage Act 1971), which of the following comments is correct?

A The offence has not been committed as this is a 'conditional' threat (if SMITH stops playing the music, the damage will not occur).

B The offence has been committed as MANNIGER intends SMITH to fear that his or another's property will be damaged.

C The offence has not been committed as SMITH does not believe MANNIGER.

D The offence has been committed as INCE believes that MANNIGER will carry out the threat and damage SMITH's car.

55. EISEMAN has been arrested for large-scale fraud relating to the use of credit cards over an extended period of time enabling him to obtain goods worth approximately £3 million. He is taken to a designated police station and a s. 18 PACE authorisation is given to search his house. When officers search the house, they recover a number of items including a computer that EISEMAN has used to carry out the fraud offences. Analysis of the computer leads to the discovery of a computer program that EISEMAN used to generate credit card numbers to carry out the fraud offences and also a computer template that EISEMAN used for producing blank utility bills when committing the fraud offences.

Does EISEMAN commit an offence of possession or control of articles for use in frauds (contrary to s. 6 of the Fraud Act 2006)?

A Yes, but only in relation to the computer program that generates credit card numbers.
B No, as these articles are related to fraud offences that have already taken place.
C Yes, in relation to the computer program that generates credit card numbers and the template that can be used for producing blank utility bills.
D No, as these items were recovered on a computer that was in EISEMAN's home.

56. CONRAD is sentenced to three years' imprisonment for an offence of burglary. He serves 18 months of the sentence and is then released. Several weeks after being released, CONRAD accompanies his friend, ZUCCARO, to a private estate where ZUCCARO is shooting (using a shotgun) in a competition. Whilst on the private estate, ZUCCARO asks CONRAD to hold on to his shotgun and a box of shotgun ammunition while he changes his clothes. CONRAD does so and several minutes later hands the shotgun and ammunition back to ZUCCARO.

Considering the law in relation to the possession of firearms by convicted persons (under s. 21 of the Firearms Act 1968), which of the comments below is correct?

A CONRAD commits an offence in relation to the shotgun and the ammunition.
B CONRAD does not commit an offence as s. 21 only applies to offenders who have been sentenced to imprisonment for five years or more.
C CONRAD commits an offence but this would only be in respect of possession of the shotgun.
D CONRAD does not commit an offence as the possession takes place on private land.

57. BONNER and WADMAN are part of a group of 25 people who share a social media account enabling them to electronically communicate with each other about their hobby (fishing). At the last fishing event the group attended, BONNER and WADMAN had an argument about cheating and the two have fallen out. BONNER believes that WADMAN is talking about him behind his back and, intending to cause WADMAN distress, he sends a message on the group social media account saying that he has evidence that WADMAN is a paedophile (this is false and BONNER knows that to be the case). WADMAN reads the social media post and laughs about it thinking that BONNER is pathetic and that nobody will believe the message. SWINNEY is part of the group of 25 and when he reads the message he believes it and it causes him anxiety as WADMAN is godfather to SWINNEY's daughter.

Does BONNER commit an offence under s. 1 of the Malicious Communications Act 1988 (malicious communication) in these circumstances?

A No, as this offence does not cover communications sent electronically.
B Yes, as soon as the communication is sent.
C No, as the message is not indecent, grossly offensive or a threat.
D Yes, but only when SWINNEY reads the message and is caused anxiety.

58. PS FLYNN is performing the role of custody officer and has authorised the detention of WILSON and SHAFIQ in relation to an offence of violent disorder; the authorisation was made at 10 pm. At that time, WILSON was very obviously intoxicated through drink and was examined by a health-care professional who stated that this was the case. SHAFIQ appeared fit and healthy. Both men were placed in cells to be interviewed at a later time.

Considering Code C in relation to the care and treatment of detained persons, which of the following statements is correct?

A WILSON should be visited and roused at least every hour; SHAFIQ should be visited at least every hour but there is no need to wake him if he is asleep.
B WILSON should be visited and roused at least every half hour; SHAFIQ should be visited at least every hour but there is no need to wake him if he is asleep.
C WILSON should be visited and roused at least every hour; SHAFIQ should be visited at least every two hours but there is no need to wake him if he is asleep.
D WILSON should be visited and roused at least every half hour; SHAFIQ should be visited at least every two hours but there is no need to wake him if he is asleep.

59. WHEELDON is attacked and robbed by REILLY (who is a stranger to WHEELDON). PC ASPEN is first to arrive at the scene of the offence and quickly obtains a first description of REILLY. PC ASPEN places WHEELDON in an unmarked police vehicle and drives WHEELDON around the local area to see if he can identify the person responsible for the offence. They drive along a busy street with a cafe on one side of the road and a pub on the other. People are outside both premises and WHEELDON is looking intently at a group outside the cafe. PC ASPEN sees a person who matches the description given by WHEELDON standing outside the pub with a group of people and asks WHEELDON to look closely at the group outside the pub. As a result, WHEELDON identifies REILLY who is in the group outside the pub and is subsequently arrested by other officers searching the area.

In relation to Code D of the Codes of Practice, which of the following comments is correct?

A Code D has not been complied with as once a first description of an offender has been obtained from a witness they should not take part in any 'street' identification process.
B Code D has not been complied with as PC ASPEN is not allowed to draw the attention of WHEELDON to a particular group.
C Code D has not been complied with as at least two officers must be present when such a 'street' identification process takes place.
D Code D of the Codes of Practice has been complied with by the officer.

60. HANRAHAN and ROE lived together for several years but the relationship ended due to HANRAHAN's violent behaviour. A year after the break up, the pair accidentally meet in a pub. HANRAHAN tells ROE that he is sorry for his past behaviour and is a changed man and wants to get back together with ROE. ROE agrees to this and the pair leave the pub and go to ROE's house where they decide to have sexual intercourse. ROE tells HANRAHAN that she will have sexual intercourse with him on the express condition that he wears a condom during sexual intercourse—HANRAHAN agrees and puts on a condom. As they get into bed together, HANRAHAN removes the condom from his penis (ROE is unaware that HANRAHAN has removed the condom) and has sexual intercourse with ROE without wearing the condom.

Considering the offence of rape (contrary to s. 1 of the Sexual Offences Act 2003), which of the following statements is correct?

A This is not an offence of rape as ROE has consented to the act of sexual intercourse.
B This is an offence of rape and the conclusive presumptions in s. 76 of the Sexual Offences Act 2003 would apply to this situation.
C This is not an offence of rape as ROE's consent to sexual intercourse was not obtained by fear or by force.
D This is an offence of rape (the issue of consent can be determined under s. 74 of the Sexual Offences Act 2003).

61. CHAPMAN (who is 14 years of age) is convicted of theft. The court decides to use its powers under s. 8 of the Crime and Disorder Act 1998 to make a parenting order in respect of GIBSON who is the guardian of CHAPMAN. In addition to the parenting order and with GIBSON's consent, the court orders GIBSON to enter into a recognisance to take proper care of CHAPMAN and exercise proper control over him (using its powers under s. 376 of the Sentencing Act 2020).

Which of the following comments is correct in relation to the parenting order and the binding over of GIBSON?

A The only reason the court may make a parenting order is because CHAPMAN has been convicted of an offence.

B A parenting order will last for a period not exceeding 12 months.

C In relation to the bind over, the maximum duration of such a recognisance is two years.

D The court must issue a bind over to GIBSON as CHAPMAN has been convicted of an offence.

62. GUNNEL and PLEYDEN agree to steal a Ferrari motor vehicle from a garage selling specialist vehicles. The plan is that GUNNEL will act as a 'look out' outside the garage while PLEYDEN breaks in and steals the car. On the evening of the offence, things are going to plan when PLEYDEN is disturbed in the garage by HENDERSON, a security guard. PLEYDEN produces a knuckleduster and assaults HENDERSON, causing him extremely serious injury in the process. The fact that PLEYDEN was in possession of a knuckleduster was unknown to GUNNEL who was only committed to stealing the Ferrari and nothing else.

With regard to the law that deals with principals and accessories, which of the following comments is correct?

A The fact that GUNNEL is present at the scene of the offence when it is committed, in itself, amounts to encouragement that would support a charge making him an accessory to the offence against HENDERSON.

B GUNNEL is liable for the injury to HENDERSON as GUNNEL and PLEYDEN have embarked on a 'joint enterprise' meaning each person is liable for the actions of the other.

C GUNNEL is not liable for the serious injuries caused to HENDERSON as PLEYDEN has done something that has gone beyond what was agreed.

D In order for an accessory to be liable for the actions of the principal, the accessory must physically take part in the offence (in this case, the harm caused to HENDERSON) and as that is not the case here, GUNNEL is not liable for the injury to HENDERSON.

63. LODWICK (aged 16 years) has been arrested in connection with the theft of a valuable painting (worth over £1 million) that has just taken place from a stately home she was visiting with her school. CCTV shows LODWICK running out of the home with the painting and passing it to someone inside a car which left the scene. LODWICK has just arrived at a designated police station and the arresting officer, PC WATERFIELD, wants to carry out an urgent interview with her without an appropriate adult being present. The officer states that any delay in interviewing LODWICK would hinder the recovery of the painting and wants to prevent that serious loss of property.

Which of the following statements is correct in relation to such an interview?

A The interview cannot take place as a juvenile cannot be interviewed without an appropriate adult being present.

B An officer of superintendent rank or above may authorise the interview in these circumstances.

C The interview cannot take place purely to prevent a serious loss of property.

D An officer of inspector rank or above may authorise the interview in these circumstances.

64. CORK has been involved in an accident whilst driving his Nissan X-Trail motor vehicle along a road. The only person who was injured in the accident was CORK and the only damage caused was to CORK's Nissan X-Trail. CORK was taken to hospital and is in an Accident and Emergency ward, as a patient at the hospital, receiving treatment for his injuries which are, as it turns out, relatively minor. PC ASKEW attends the hospital intending to ask CORK to take part in a preliminary breath test under s. 6(5) of the Road Traffic Act 1988.

Can PC ASKEW require CORK to cooperate with a preliminary breath test in this situation?

A No, not unless the medical practitioner in immediate charge of CORK's case has been notified of the proposal to make the requirement and does not object to the requirement being carried out.

B Yes, as long as PC ASKEW is in uniform.

C No, as the only person injured was CORK and the only vehicle damaged was CORK's vehicle, this is not an 'accident'.

D Yes, and if CORK fails the test he can be arrested under s. 6D of the Road Traffic Act 1988.

65. PC CARRIGAN attends a house where it is reported that TOPHAM (a child aged 16) has been suffering ill-treatment and neglect at the hands of her foster-parent. PC CARRIGAN sees TOPHAM and speaks to her and concludes that the allegations appear to be true. Believing that TOPHAM would otherwise be likely to suffer significant harm, the officer uses the powers under s. 46 of the Children Act 1989 and takes TOPHAM into 'police protection'.

Is this a lawful use of the powers available under s. 46 of the Children Act 1989?

A No, as TOPHAM is 16 years old.

B Yes, but the maximum period of time TOPHAM could spend in 'police protection' is 72 hours.

C No, an officer of the rank of inspector or above must authorise the use of the power.

D Yes, and PC CARRIGAN can also carry out the role of the 'designated officer' in these circumstances.

66. FOGARTY attends a police station at the request of PC MARRI. PC MARRI believes FOGARTY to be a witness to an offence of theft and wishes to ask FOGARTY some questions about the offence. FOGARTY arrives at the police station and, as soon as PC MARRI begins to speak to him, he tells the officer that he is not a witness and that he actually committed the offence of theft. PC MARRI considers it is necessary to arrest FOGARTY and does so.

Could FOGARTY be searched using the powers under s. 32 of the Police and Criminal Evidence Act 1984?

A Yes, but only for anything which FOGARTY might use to assist him to escape from lawful custody.

B No, as s. 32 is a power to search premises where the arrested person has been prior to arrest and not a power to search the arrested person.

C Yes, but only for anything which might be evidence relating to an offence.

D No, as FOGARTY has been arrested at a police station.

67. PERRYMAN (a UK national) facilitates the travel of ARVANITE (an Albanian national) with a view to ARVANITE being exploited. PERRYMAN is arrested and charged with an offence of human trafficking (under s. 2 of the Modern Slavery Act 2015). PERRYMAN pleads 'guilty' to the offence which is dealt with by a magistrates' court. PERRYMAN is sentenced to four months' imprisonment for the offence.

Could a slavery and trafficking prevention order (under s. 14 of the Modern Slavery Act 2015) be imposed on PERRYMAN in this situation?

A Yes, and the order will last for a fixed period of at least three years or until a further order is made.

B No, slavery and trafficking prevention orders can only be imposed when an offender has been convicted of a slavery or trafficking offence and the court has determined that a sentence of four years or more is appropriate.

C Yes, and, if necessary, the order may prohibit PERRYMAN travelling to any country outside the United Kingdom.

D No, slavery and trafficking prevention orders can only be made by a Crown Court or the Court of Appeal.

68. MOSS wants to have sexual intercourse with a prostitute. He is aware that East House Road (which is about three miles from his home) has a strong reputation for prostitution activities and he gets into his car and drives to the location. MOSS drives up and down East House Road for 10 minutes and can see that there are a number of women standing outside the front door of a house on the road. MOSS makes the assumption that they are all prostitutes and pulls up next to the women in his car. He lowers the passenger window and speaks to one of the women, DOWELL. MOSS asks, *'How much for a fuck?'* DOWELL is not a prostitute and is in fact going out for the night with her friends. She tells MOSS to *'Drop dead!'* MOSS gets out of his car and walks up to DOWELL and says, *'C'mon, don't play hard to get. How much for a shag?'* DOWELL threatens to call the police and MOSS gets into his car and drives away.

With regard to the offence of soliciting by 'kerb-crawling' (contrary to s. 51A of the Sexual Offences Act 2003), which of the following comments is correct?

A The offence is committed the moment MOSS first solicits DOWELL (when he is inside his car).

B The offence has not been committed unless it can be shown that the soliciting by MOSS was likely to cause nuisance or annoyance to others.

C The offence is committed but only when MOSS approaches DOWELL on foot.

D The offence has not been committed as DOWELL is not a prostitute.

69. ZHONG has been arrested for offences relating to fraud and has been bailed to appear at a magistrates' court with several bail conditions including the provision of a surety; ZHONG's surety is GEDDES. Once he is released, ZHONG tells GEDDES that he has no intention of surrendering to the custody of the court and is going to escape to China. GEDDES writes to the police telling them of ZHONG's plan and that he no longer wishes to be a surety. PC LOW is the officer in charge of the case and is told about the situation. PC LOW visits ZHONG's home address and arrests him under s. 7 of the Bail Act 1976 based on the information the police received in the letter sent by GEDDES.

In relation to s. 7 of the Bail Act 1976 (the liability to arrest for absconding or breaking bail conditions), which of the following comments is correct?

A PC LOW should not have arrested ZHONG as ZHONG has not failed to surrender to the custody of the court or broken any bail conditions.

B ZHONG should be charged with an offence of breaking his bail conditions (under s. 7 of the Act) and brought before a court within 24 hours of his arrest.

C ZHONG should be brought before a judge of the Crown Court as soon as practicable.

D ZHONG must be dealt with by a justice as soon as practicable and in any case within 24 hours of being arrested.

70. ROSS works as a clerk for a large car sales firm. She is examining a number of expenses claims (required for accounting purposes) that have been submitted by FINLAY (a supervisor at the car sales firm). ROSS discovers a significant number of irregularities suggesting that expenses amounting to £3,000 are false and she confronts FINLAY regarding the irregularities. FINLAY admits the expenses are false but threatens ROSS to the effect that if she does anything about the false claims he will make sure that she loses her job, and he tells ROSS to falsify the expenses claims so that they appear genuine. FINLAY has a great deal of influence at the firm and ROSS honestly believes he could get her sacked. ROSS fears that this loss of income will have a dramatic impact on her standard of living and she falsifies the expenses for FINLAY.

Would ROSS be able to claim that she was acting under duress of circumstances in relation to any offences that she commits by falsifying the expenses claims?

A No, as she did not have cause to fear she that would suffer death or serious injury if she did not do as FINLAY demanded.

B Yes, as the defence is available in answer to any charge except for treason.

C No, as duress of circumstances is only a defence to a charge of murder or attempted murder.

D Yes, because she honestly believed that she would be sacked if she did not do as FINLAY demanded.

71. PC STAS is on uniform mobile patrol and checks a car driven by OWEN. The check reveals that there is no insurance in place for the car. PC STAS attempts to stop the car but it drives off at speed. PC STAS makes further enquiries regarding the car and establishes the address where the car is registered to OWEN. PC STAS visits the address two days later and sees the vehicle on the driveway of the address (a private dwelling).

Can PC STAS seize the car using the power under s. 165A of the Road Traffic Act 1988?

A No, as 48 hours have passed since the time the incident took place.

B Yes, and PC STAS may use reasonable force in order to do so.

C No, as it is on the driveway of a private dwelling.

D Yes, the car may be seized at any time within 72 hours following the incident.

72. Jane TURNER has suffered years of abuse at the hands of Paul TURNER (her husband). One evening, Paul attacks Jane and is in the process of punching her about the body when Jane reacts in self-defence and picks up a knife and stabs and kills Paul. ARTHERN (a neighbour of the TURNERs) had heard the noise of the attack and walks into the TURNERs' house and sees Jane standing over the body of Paul holding the knife in her hand. ARTHERN asks Jane, *'Did you kill him?'* In response, Jane nods her head. PC EDDOWES is the first police officer at the scene and walks into the lounge of the house. On seeing the officer, Jane states *'He left me no choice—I was defending myself, officer!'*

Considering the law regarding confessions under s. 82 of the Police and Criminal Evidence Act 1984, which of the following comments is correct?

A Jane's response to the question posed by ARTHERN would not be a confession as it was not made in words.

B Jane's response to the question posed by ARTHERN would not be a confession; the statement made to PC EDDOWES would be.

C Jane's response to the question posed by ARTHERN and the statement made to PC EDDOWES would both be confessions.

D Jane's response to the question posed by ARTHERN would not be a confession as it was not made to a person in authority.

73. BALL and six of his friends plan to attend a designated football match between Manchester United and Arsenal at Old Trafford (the home ground of Manchester United). BALL hires a Ford Galaxy SMVR (which seats seven people including the driver) to transport them from London to Manchester. BALL drives the vehicle and picks up his six friends outside a pub. HAMES (who is part of the group of six) places boxes containing cans of lager in the rear of the Ford Galaxy. KEASEY (also part of the group) is already drunk when the group are picked up by BALL. He climbs into the vehicle and falls asleep straight away. BALL is aware that the lager has been placed in the rear of the vehicle and that KEASEY is drunk. The group then set off to Manchester.

Who, if anyone, has committed an offence under s. 1A of the Sporting Events (Control of Alcohol etc.) Act 1985 (alcohol on other vehicles)?

A The offence has not been committed in these circumstances.

B Only BALL commits the offence.

C BALL and HAMES commit the offence.

D BALL, HAMES and KEASEY commit the offence.

74. ANSELL commits an offence of blackmail (contrary to s. 21 of the Theft Act 1968). The blackmail nets ANSELL £5,000 in cash. ANSELL places the money into his bank account and then transfers it into the account of his friend, GARNER. GARNER is thoroughly aware of the source of the money but this does not stop him holding on to the money. Two months later, ANSELL asks for the money to be returned to him and GARNER withdraws the cash.

Does GARNER commit an offence of dishonestly retaining a wrongful credit (contrary to s. 24A of the Theft Act 1968)?

A No, as a credit to an account is not 'wrongful' for the purposes of this offence if it derives from an offence of blackmail.

B Yes, the offence is committed when GARNER fails to take steps to cancel the credit.

C No, as 'wrongful credits' relate to accidental credits made to an account that are then dishonestly retained.

D Yes, as long as the £5,000 placed in his account means that the account is in 'credit' (rather than being overdrawn) after the credit has been made.

75. CHESTERFIELD is HIV-positive and is aware of that fact. One afternoon, CHESTERFIELD is speaking to D'SOUZA (his neighbour) and she confesses that she has always wanted to have sex with him. She invites CHESTERFIELD into her house where she tells CHESTERFIELD that she wants to have sexual intercourse with him. CHESTERFIELD believes that if he uses a condom the risk of him passing the HIV virus to D'SOUZA, although still possible, will be significantly reduced and on that basis he has protected sexual intercourse with D'SOUZA (penis to vagina) using a condom. A few days later, D'SOUZA is told by another neighbour that CHESTERFIELD is carrying the HIV virus. D'SOUZA visits a police station and reports that she has been raped, stating that she would not have had sex with CHESTERFIELD had she known he was carrying the HIV virus. A later analysis of D'SOUZA's blood reveals that she is HIV-positive (this can be traced back to her sexual activity with CHESTERFIELD).

Which of the following statements is correct in relation to CHESTERFIELD's liability?

A CHESTERFIELD would be guilty of recklessly causing D'SOUZA grievous bodily harm (contrary to s. 20 of the Offences Against the Person Act 1861).

B CHESTERFIELD would be guilty of assault (contrary to s. 47 of the Offences Against the Person Act 1861).

C CHESTERFIELD commits rape (contrary to s. 1 of the Sexual Offences Act 2003) in these circumstances as he did not tell D'SOUZA that he was HIV-positive.

D CHESTERFIELD would be guilty of rape (contrary to s. 1 of the Sexual Offences Act 2003) if he had not taken measures to protect D'SOUZA by wearing a condom.

76. DAVIS is an extremely violent criminal who is part of a gang distributing drugs. DAVIS is arrested for firearms offences and is in police custody at a designated police station and will be interviewed about the offences on video. One of the interviewing officers, DC HAMBLETON, has expert knowledge of the activities of the gang and for that reason the officer in charge of the investigation into the activities of the gang wants DC HAMBLETON to interview DAVIS. DC HAMBLETON tells the officer in charge of the case that he reasonably believes that providing his name during the course of the interview would put him in danger.

Considering the guidance provided by Codes E and F of the Codes of Practice on such matters, which of the following comments is correct?

A The interview should take place as normal but DC HAMBLETON should only provide his warrant number (instead of his name).

B A screen can be provided so that DC HAMBLETON cannot be seen by DAVIS during the course of the interview.

C If an officer of the rank of at least inspector certifies that it is necessary for the officer's safety, DC HAMBLETON should give his warrant number (instead of his name) and also state the police station to which he is attached.

D DC HAMBLETON can take part in the interview but should have his back to the camera and give his warrant number (not his name) and the name of the police station to which he is attached.

77. DARLOW finds out that his girlfriend (TOOMER) is having an affair with his best friend (GUTHRIE). DARLOW decides that he will get revenge on the pair by causing them really serious harm and plans to wait until they are having sex with each other and to burst in on them and throw strong acid over the pair. His intention is to cause them horrific burn injuries that will scar them for the rest of their lives. As DARLOW works in a laboratory, he has access to chemicals and obtains a container of hydrofluoric acid. He pretends to go to work and waits until he sees GUTHRIE visit his house. He sneaks into the house and bursts into a bedroom where TOOMER and GUTHRIE are having sexual intercourse and he shakes the acid container towards the pair. But as DARLOW was so emotional he forgot to take off the top of the container and no harm is caused to TOOMER or GUTHRIE.

Does DARLOW commit an offence of attempted murder (contrary to s. 1 of the Criminal Attempts Act 1981) in this situation?

A No, as DARLOW does not intend to kill TOOMER and GUTHRIE.

B No, it is impossible for the offence to be committed (the top has not been removed from the container).

C Yes, when he bursts into the bedroom.

D Yes, when he shakes the container towards TOOMER and GUTHRIE.

78. FIELD is a 12-year-old girl and is attracted to her piano teacher, McNULTY, who provides private tuition to FIELD at his home address. For some time, FIELD's mother accompanied her to her lessons; however, as FIELD has been having lessons for three years with McNULTY, her mother now allows her to go on her own. FIELD is physically well developed for her age, however McNULTY is aware of her true age. During a piano lesson, FIELD asks McNULTY to touch her legs up to her pants. McNULTY flatly refuses and tells her not to be so silly. FIELD says to McNULTY, *'Well, I really want you to have sex with me, to be my first.'* At this, she stands up and removes her pants; McNULTY, shocked and worried, leaves the room immediately.

Considering s. 44 of the Serious Crime Act 2007 (intentionally encouraging or assisting an offence), is FIELD liable?

A FIELD is not guilty in these circumstances as rape would be committed if McNULTY had sex with her, which is for her own protection.

B FIELD does commit the offence as she is over the age of 10 years, the age of criminal responsibility.

C FIELD is not guilty in these circumstances as the act she encouraged did not take place.

D FIELD is guilty of the offence but in the circumstances it would be an attempt owing to her age being under 13.

79. BROOKER (aged 17 years) is at her parents' home and looking after her child (who is 2 years old). BROOKER is feeling depressed as she feels she has no future career prospects so, to make herself feel a little better about things, she is smoking cannabis (which she does not possess legally). BROOKER smokes a significant amount of cannabis and under the influence of the drug she falls asleep on a settee in the lounge of the house. BROOKER rolls onto her 2-year-old child (who is sleeping next to BROOKER on the settee) and causes the death of her child via suffocation.

In relation to the offence of child cruelty (under s. 1 of the Children and Young Persons Act 1933), which of the following comments is correct?

A The offence has not been committed as the suffocation did not take place when BROOKER was 'in bed' with her child.

B BROOKER can be charged with the offence of child cruelty even though her child has died.

C BROOKER has not committed the offence as she is 17 years old.

D The offence is committed when the person suffocates the child when under the influence of drink; in this situation, BROOKER would not commit the offence.

80. KENYON is sitting in the driver's seat of a Honda Civic motor vehicle which is parked in the car park of a pub. There are no barriers preventing access to the pub car park which is open to pub customers. The licensee has called the police as he has seen KENYON smoking what he suspects is cannabis. PC COBB (on uniform mobile patrol) attends the scene and speaks with KENYON who slurs his responses to the officer. PC COBB can smell cannabis and, because of the slurred responses to his questions and the smell of the drug, he reasonably suspects that KENYON is under the influence of cannabis and has committed an offence under s. 5A(1)(b) of the Road Traffic Act 1988 (being in charge of a motor vehicle with a concentration of a specified drug above the specified limit).

Based on these facts, can PC COBB arrest KENYON using his power of arrest under s. 6D of the Road Traffic Act 1988?

   A Yes, but only because the officer is in uniform.
   B No, because the pub car park is a public place and the arrest powers under s. 6D are only available when an offence has taken place on a road.
   C Yes, the suspicion that KENYON is under the influence of a drug would be enough to allow the use of the power of arrest under s. 6D.
   D No, because KENYON has not taken and failed a preliminary drug test or failed to cooperate with a preliminary drug test.

81. DUFFY is driving a Vauxhall Astra along a road in an erratic manner. DC STAMP (dressed in plain clothes and driving an unmarked police vehicle) is behind DUFFY and witnesses the poor driving. DUFFY reaches a set of traffic lights and stops his vehicle. DC STAMP gets out of his vehicle and approaches DUFFY. He identifies himself as a police officer and speaks to DUFFY. DUFFY's responses are slurred and DC STAMP forms the opinion that he is unfit to drive and arrests DUFFY for the offence of driving whilst unfit (contrary to s. 4(1) of the Road Traffic Act 1988). DC STAMP reaches through the car door to take hold of DUFFY; DUFFY has no intention of allowing the officer to arrest and detain him so he slams the car door on the officer's arm, breaking DC STAMP's arm in the process. DUFFY did not intend to break the officer's arm, just to stop the officer arresting him, although he did realise that slamming the door on the officer's arm would cause some harm to the officer.

Considering the liability of DUFFY in relation to offences against the person, which of the comments below is correct?

   A DUFFY is not liable for any offence as the arrest the officer made was unlawful.
   B DUFFY has committed a s. 47 battery offence.
   C DUFFY has committed a s. 20 grievous bodily harm offence.
   D DUFFY has committed a s. 18 grievous bodily harm offence.

82. PCs PRENTICE and FELLOWES are on uniform mobile patrol when they are called to a disturbance outside a pub. When they arrive, VICKER is standing outside the pub shouting and swearing very loudly. The officers cannot calm VICKER down and have no choice but to arrest him for a public order offence. On arrest, VICKER becomes extremely violent towards the officers and is resisting the arrest with all his might. The incident has drawn a crowd of 10 people from the pub. In the crowd are HARLOW and GREEN who both hate the police. While VICKER struggles, HARLOW shouts out *'We'll help you mate, we'll kick their fuckin' heads in!'* and GREEN kicks out at PC FELLOWES but misses. He kicks out again but this time at the door of the police vehicle the officers arrived in and he dents the door. Other officers arrive and VICKER is taken from the scene. HARLOW and GREEN are also arrested. All three men are later charged with the offence of violent disorder (contrary to s. 2 of the Public Order Act 1986).

Which of the following statements is correct?

A The offence of violent disorder has been committed by all three men in this scenario.
B The offence has not been committed as the three men did not act deliberately in combination with each other.
C The offence of violent disorder has not been committed as GREEN's conduct was towards property not a person and this does not satisfy the requirement for 'unlawful violence'.
D The offence has not been committed as three or more people must actually use violence for a conviction to be secured.

83. MAXWELL visits a large agricultural show held in the private grounds of a country home—entry to the show and grounds is open to members of the public who pay a £5 entry fee. MAXWELL is seen behaving in a suspicious manner near to several luxury cars on a display stand and the manager of the display is concerned and contacts the police who have posted several officers to the show. PCs WALGRAVE and AHMAD visit the stand and as they get closer to it they see MAXWELL walking towards them. They stop MAXWELL and carry out a lawful search under s. 1 of the Police and Criminal Evidence Act 1984. During the course of the search, they search a bag MAXWELL is carrying and inside that bag they find a single shot 'airsoft gun' (which has a kinetic energy level of 1.34 joules) and a telescopic sight for a rifle (not the airsoft gun in MAXWELL's bag). MAXWELL tells the officers that he does not possess a firearms certificate of any description.

Does MAXWELL commit an offence of possession of a firearm in a public place (contrary to s. 19 of the Firearms Act 1968)?

A Yes, but only in relation to the airsoft gun.
B No, it is not an offence to possess an airsoft gun of this type (it is not a firearm), nor is it an offence to possess a telescopic sight for a rifle (it is not a firearm).
C Yes, but only in relation to the telescopic sight for the rifle.
D No, MAXWELL is not in a public place.

84. Adrian and Gary BLENKINSOP are fraternal twins and are of roughly similar appearance. The pair carry out an offence of robbery and are arrested in connection with it but both dispute the eye-witness identification evidence. The identification officer and the officer in charge of the case consult each other and because a video identification is not practicable, it is decided to offer Adrian and Gary BLENKINSOP an identification parade.

Considering the requirements of Annex B of Code D of the Codes of Practice and the identification parade procedure, could Adrian and Gary BLENKINSOP be paraded together?

A No, Adrian and Gary BLENKINSOP must take part in separate identification parades.
B Yes, Adrian and Gary BLENKINSOP may be paraded together with at least 12 other people.
C No, unless an officer of the rank of inspector or above certifies that it is expedient to do so.
D Yes, Adrian and Gary BLENKINSOP may be paraded together with at least 16 other people.

85. HINCHCLIFFE is lying on a sun lounger in her private rear garden, wearing a bikini and sunbathing. STODDART, who is HINCHCLIFFE's next-door neighbour, sees HINCHCLIFFE and is outraged by her behaviour as she believes HINCHCLIFFE is trying to seduce her husband and that this activity is part of a bigger plan. She leans over the fence separating the rear gardens and shouts *'Whore!'* at HINCHCLIFFE. HINCHCLIFFE thinks STODDART is an idiot and, intending to cause STODDART alarm and distress, she rips off her bikini top and exposes her breasts to STODDART. She immediately follows this act by standing up, pulling her bikini pants down and exposing her buttocks ('mooning') to STODDART shouting *'Kiss my arse, you silly old bag!'*

Does HINCHCLIFFE commit an offence of exposure (contrary to s. 66 of the Sexual Offences Act 1968)?

A No, as this offence requires the activity to be carried out for the purposes of sexual gratification rather than to cause alarm or distress.
B Yes, exposing the buttocks and the female breasts with intent to cause alarm or distress would amount to an offence.
C No, as HINCHCLIFFE did not expose her genitals to STODDART.
D Yes, although the buttocks are not included, exposing the female breasts with intent to cause alarm or distress amounts to an offence.

86. A protest is to take place regarding immigration. A large amount of intelligence has been received about the protest which includes information to the effect that a number of the protesters will be wearing masks and other items to wholly or mainly conceal their identity, enabling them to commit offences without being identified. At a similar protest march a few weeks earlier, several public order and assault offences took place and the offenders all wore items concealing their identity. As a result of this information, an authorisation under s. 60AA of the Criminal Justice and Public Order Act 1994 is given.

In relation to such an authorisation, which of the following comments is correct?

A The initial authorisation will last for a maximum period of 12 hours.
B The power under s. 60AA is only available to police officers in uniform.
C The power under s. 60AA allows police officers to search persons and vehicles for items that might be used wholly or mainly to conceal identity.
D After the initial authorisation period has ended, the power cannot be extended.

87. PC DUFFY is subject to a complaint and the investigation of the complaint has led to a misconduct meeting taking place.

In relation to that misconduct meeting, and in particular the timing of the misconduct meeting, which of the following comments is correct?

A The misconduct meeting shall take place not later than 20 working days beginning with the first working day after the date on which the documents and material for the meeting were supplied to PC DUFFY; this time limit may not be extended.
B The misconduct meeting shall take place not later than 28 working days beginning with the first working day after the date on which the documents and material for the meeting were supplied to PC DUFFY; this time limit may not be extended.
C The misconduct meeting shall take place not later than 20 working days beginning with the first working day after the date on which the documents and material for the meeting were supplied to PC DUFFY; this time limit may be extended.
D The misconduct meeting shall take place not later than 28 working days beginning with the first working day after the date on which the documents and material for the meeting were supplied to PC DUFFY; this time limit may be extended.

88. PC PLATTEN is on uniform mobile patrol and is driving along a road directly behind an Audi TT motor vehicle driven by GREY. GREY indicates left and turns into the private drive of his house but once on the drive he swerves, leaves the drive, drives onto his front lawn and collides with some garden furniture on his front lawn. This causes damage to GREY's vehicle and the garden furniture belonging to GREY. PC PLATTEN stops and speaks to GREY who is unsteady on his feet and smells strongly of intoxicants. As a result of his observations of GREY, PC PLATTEN reasonably suspects that GREY is drunk.

Could PC PLATTEN require GREY to cooperate with a preliminary test under s. 6 of the Road Traffic Act 1988?

   A Yes, if the officer reasonably suspects GREY has been driving a motor vehicle on a road while having alcohol in his body and still has alcohol in his body.
   B No, GREY has not been involved in a reportable accident.
   C Yes, but only because the officer is in uniform.
   D No, nobody has been injured as a consequence of the accident.

89. BOTHAM has acrimoniously split up with ZAPPE (his long-time girlfriend) and there is a nasty feud between them regarding access to their 6-month-old baby. BOTHAM is chatting to a friend of his on a street corner when he sees ZAPPE walking towards him holding their baby in her arms. Seeing ZAPPE is too much for BOTHAM who loses his temper and runs up to ZAPPE and punches her in the face causing her to lose consciousness for several seconds and fall to the ground causing significant bruising to her face (a more than transient injury). The force of the blow causes ZAPPE to drop the baby and consequently the baby is caused slight injury when it hits the pavement (some minor bruising to the baby's arm).

Thinking about the law relating to offences of assault (particularly the offences of assault contrary to s. 39 of the Criminal Justice Act 1988 and s. 47 of the Offences Against the Person Act 1861), which of the following comments is correct?

   A BOTHAM has committed a s. 39 offence against ZAPPE and also the 6-month-old baby (a battery in both cases).
   B BOTHAM has committed a s. 39 battery offence against ZAPPE but no offence in relation to the 6-month-old baby.
   C BOTHAM has committed a s. 47 assault against ZAPPE and the 6-month-old baby.
   D BOTHAM has committed a s. 47 assault against ZAPPE and a s. 39 offence (a battery) against the 6-month-old baby.

90. DC JELF is investigating an offence of sexual assault (under s. 3 of the Sexual Offences Act 2003) that took place in Wood Street last Saturday evening. The officer believes that there may well be a number of untraced witnesses to the offence and wishes to identify them by carrying out a road check (under s. 4 of the Police and Criminal Evidence Act 1984) in Wood Street this coming Saturday evening. DC JELF approaches Inspector VIVIER and asks for his authorisation for a road check to take place.

Can Inspector VIVIER authorise a road check in these circumstances?

A No, as a road check cannot be authorised to ascertain whether a vehicle is carrying a witness to an indictable offence, only a person who has committed such an offence.

B Yes, and if authorised it will last for a period not exceeding seven days.

C No, it must be authorised by an officer of the rank of superintendent or above.

D Yes, but the authorisation must be in writing.

91. ARBUTHNOTT is 13 years old and is at a designated police station having been arrested for an offence of burglary. The officer in the case is DC CRAWLEY who is considering taking footwear impressions from the shoes worn by ARBUTHNOTT as part of her investigation into the burglary offence (no footwear impressions have been taken in the course of the investigation).

In relation to such footwear impressions, which of the following statements is correct?

A Footwear impressions could only be obtained with the written consent of ARBUTHNOTT and an appropriate adult.

B Footwear impressions could be obtained but DC CRAWLEY would require the consent of ARBUTHNOTT's appropriate adult.

C No consent is required as ARBUTHNOTT has been arrested in connection with a 'recordable' offence.

D Footwear impressions cannot be taken from ARBUTHNOTT as he is under the age of 14.

92. PC CURTIS is on uniform foot patrol when she is directed to an incident involving an offence of assault. PC CURTIS arrives at the scene of the offence and, as a result of information received, she arrests HYNDE on suspicion of committing assault. As PC CURTIS is on her own, she asks for another officer to attend the scene but is informed that no other officers are available to do so. The officer is concerned that she will not be able to take HYNDE to a designated police station without HYNDE injuring her so she decides to take HYNDE to a non-designated police station which is a three-minute walk from the scene of the arrest.

Considering s. 30 of the Police and Criminal Evidence Act 1984, which of the following comments is correct?

A The officer has behaved unlawfully as all arrested persons must be taken to a designated police station as soon as practicable after the arrest. There are no exceptions to this requirement.

B The behaviour of PC CURTIS is lawful but HYNDE should be taken to a designated police station not more than six hours after his arrival at the first police station unless he is released previously.

C The officer has behaved unlawfully as the only justification for taking an arrested person to a non-designated police station after arrest is if it appears to the constable that the arrested person will injure him/herself, the constable or some other person.

D The behaviour of PC CURTIS is lawful as long as, after arriving at the non-designated police station, she contacts an officer of the rank of inspector or above to inform him/her of her actions. In such a case, the arrested person will be taken to a designated police station as soon as is practicable.

93. DUBAR has been charged with an offence of handling stolen goods (contrary to s. 22 of the Theft Act 1968). DUBAR has a previous conviction for theft which precedes the date of the handling offence by four years. The police also have evidence that DUBAR had stolen property in his possession from a theft that preceded the handling offence by nine months (he was never charged with an offence relating to that incident).

Which of the following comments is correct in respect of the ability of the prosecution to utilise s. 27 of the Theft Act 1968 (admissibility of previous misconduct for the purpose of proving DUBAR knew or believed the goods to be stolen goods)?

A Provided that seven days' notice in writing is given to DUBAR, the previous conviction is admissible as is the evidence that he was in possession of stolen property nine months ago.

B Provided that seven days' notice in writing is given to DUBAR, the previous conviction is admissible; the evidence that he was in possession of stolen property nine months ago is inadmissible.

C The previous conviction is inadmissible; the evidence that he was in possession of stolen property nine months ago is admissible.

D The previous conviction and the evidence that he was in possession of stolen property nine months ago are both inadmissible.

94. FISHER has attended a designated police station at the request of PC JAKEMAN to take part in a voluntary interview regarding an allegation of theft. It is PC JAKEMAN's intention that the interview will be audio recorded but when FISHER arrives at the police station, the two interview rooms at the police station are unavailable (one of the rooms has a fault with the recording equipment and the other is being used to interview a suspect and will not be available for some time).

If a written record of the interview is to be made, who would be the 'relevant officer' in these circumstances?

A An officer of the rank of inspector or above.
B The custody officer at the designated police station.
C An officer of the rank of sergeant or above.
D PC JAKEMAN (the interviewing officer).

95. DIXON is arrested in Glasgow (Scotland) at 22.20hrs on Tuesday evening on behalf of Hampshire Police who want to question DIXON in relation to an offence of s. 18 wounding (Offences Against the Person Act 1861). DCs SHEPPARD and ECKLEY (Hampshire police officers) are sent to Scotland to pick up DIXON and bring him back to Portsmouth police station. The officers arrive in Glasgow the day after DIXON was arrested (Wednesday) at 09.00hrs. They transport DIXON to Portsmouth crossing the border between England and Scotland at 10.30hrs that day. They stop in Birmingham at 14.00hrs that day to obtain refreshments (during this time DIXON is lodged in a cell block in Birmingham city centre). They recommence their journey and enter the Hampshire police area at 16.30hrs and arrive at Portsmouth police station at 17.30hrs.

What would DIXON's 'relevant time' be in this situation?

A 22.20hrs on Tuesday.
B 10.30hrs on Wednesday.
C 16.30hrs on Wednesday.
D 17.30hrs on Wednesday.

96. PC CHARLESWORTH attends the scene of a disturbance where it has been reported that two men are arguing in the street. When the officer arrives, he sees OAKMAN and PRITCHARD shouting at each other. The officer approaches the two men and asks them to calm down, at which point OAKMAN says '*Fuck off, copper!*' and PRITCHARD says '*Mind your own business, pig!*' HALSTEAD (an off-duty police officer) is walking past the incident and, hearing the abuse, walks over to PC CHARLESWORTH, identifies himself and offers to help deal with the situation. Hearing this, OAKMAN punches HALSTEAD in the face (causing a small cut to HALSTEAD's lip) and PRITCHARD kicks PC CHARLESWORTH on the left shin (causing minor bruising). In both cases, the injuries are slight.

Would the Assaults on Emergency Workers (Offences) Act 2019 be relevant to the assaults on PCs CHARLESWORTH and HALSTEAD?

A No, the legislation is not relevant in this situation as it only applies to offences under s. 18 of the Offences Against the Person Act 1861.

B Yes, but only PC CHARLESWORTH would be subject to the legislation.

C No, the legislation is not relevant in this situation as it only applies to offences under ss. 47, 20 and 18 of the Offences Against the Person Act 1861.

D Yes, the legislation would be relevant to PCs CHARLESWORTH and HALSTEAD.

97. Inspector THOMAS is delivering a training course for newly promoted sergeants and inspectors—part of the course deals with the law in relation to the Equality Act 2010 and in particular the 'protected characteristics' covered by the Act. During a class discussion in relation to those protected characteristics and case law surrounding the issue, a number of comments are made.

In relation to the comments made by members of the class, which one shows a correct understanding of Equality Act 2010 law?

A When discussing the protected characteristic of disability (s. 6 of the Act), a member of the class states that people who have a disability are protected against discrimination; those who have had a disability are not protected.

B When discussing the protected characteristic of religion or belief (s. 10 of the Act), a member of the class states that a person holding gender-critical beliefs (that sex is immutable) would have this characteristic.

C When discussing the protected characteristic of marriage and civil partnership (s. 8 of the Act), a member of the class states that opposite-sex couples in a civil partnership do not have this characteristic.

D When discussing the protected characteristic of race (s. 9 of the Act), a member of the class states that as Scots, Welsh and English persons are ethnic groups, they would have this characteristic.

98. HEMMING is the licensee of 'The Crooked Man' pub. It is his birthday and, when the pub is closed, he has a private celebration in the lounge of the pub with his best friend WILLIAMSON. The two men become exceptionally drunk and use a karaoke machine so loudly that neighbours complain and the police are called to the pub. PC WHITE attends the pub and finds the two men in the lounge of the pub, drunk and singing loudly.

Has the offence of being found drunk (contrary to s. 12 of the Licensing Act 1872) been committed in these circumstances?

A Yes, but only WILLIAMSON would commit the offence in these circumstances.
B No, as this offence only applies to licensed premises when they are open to the public.
C Yes, HEMMING and WILLIAMSON have committed the offence.
D No, as the men are not found drunk in any highway or public place.

99. ACTON and MOORECROFT work in the same office but do not get on with each other. ACTON tampers with MOORECROFT's office chair so that when MOORECROFT sits on it, the back of the chair will give way causing MOORECROFT to fall on the floor. ACTON realises THAT this may cause some harm to MOORECROFT but considers the risk to be a reasonable one as any harm will only be slight (perhaps some minor bruising). MOORECROFT sits on the chair, falls off and breaks his arm. ACTON is charged with a s. 20 offence (contrary to the Offences Against the Person Act 1861).

Considering the issues surrounding the concept of recklessness as they apply to the s. 20 offence, which of the following statements is correct?

A ACTON is not 'reckless' for the purposes of this offence as he did not foresee the risk that serious harm would be caused to MOORECROFT.
B Whether ACTON was 'reckless' or not will be considered by the court/jury asking whether a reasonable bystander would have been aware of the risk of some injury being caused to MOORECROFT.
C ACTON is 'reckless' for the purposes of the s. 20 offence as he foresaw the risk that some harm would befall MOORECROFT.
D As ACTON considered the risk a reasonable one, he will not be 'reckless'.

100. THIRLWELL is in police custody at a designated police station having been arrested in connection with an offence of importing a controlled drug. THIRLWELL was interviewed regarding the offence by DS McNALLY (the officer in the case) and her colleague DC GREENSMITH. THIRLWELL denied the offence and, in particular, disputes the evidence of several eye-witnesses. Due to the seriousness of the case, it is decided to hold an identification parade whilst THIRLWELL is in police custody. However, there is difficulty locating an inspector to act as an 'identification officer' which is causing an unreasonable delay to the investigation.

In relation to such a situation, which of the following comments correctly sets out the procedure that should be followed?

A The explanation of the identification procedure and notice in relation to it could be provided to THIRLWELL by the custody officer (who is not involved in the investigation).

B The explanation of the identification procedure and the notice in relation to it must be provided to THIRLWELL by an officer of the rank of inspector or above who is not involved in the investigation.

C The explanation of the identification procedure and the notice in relation to it could be provided to THIRLWELL by DS McNALLY but not by DC GREENSMITH.

D The explanation of the identification procedure and notice in relation to it could be provided to THIRLWELL by DS McNALLY or DC GREENSMITH.

101. HODGSON is driving a Land Rover motor vehicle and towing a caravan. He drives onto a field owned by EGERTON and sets up to camp on the field (trespassing in the field). EGERTON sees this and contacts the police and PC YASAR (an officer on uniform patrol) attends the scene where EGERTON asks the officer to remove HODGSON from his land. PC YASAR speaks to HODGSON who tells the officer that he is from the travelling community and intends to camp on the land for three days. PC YASAR establishes that there is a suitable pitch on a relevant caravan site for HODGSON's caravan at a nearby local authority camping site.

Can PC YASAR direct HODGSON to leave the site using the power under s. 62A of the Criminal Justice and Public Order Act 1994?

A Yes, but only because the officer is in uniform.

B No, EGERTON has not taken reasonable steps to ask HODGSON to leave.

C Yes, if an inspector or above authorises it, the direction to leave can be communicated by any constable at the scene.

D No, as there is only one person (HODGSON) trespassing on the land.

102. STOCK commits an offence of theft from a supermarket. The police are called and PC BURN attends the scene and arrests STOCK. STOCK struggles against the arrest and HALEEM (a customer in the supermarket) sees this and does nothing to help the officer. PC BURN shouts out for help and HALEEM decides to assist the officer deal with STOCK, and he runs over and joins the struggle. As all three are pulling and pushing in opposite directions, it actually turns out that HALEEM is of no help to PC BURN and HALEEM's intervention actually enables STOCK to escape from the supermarket.

Does HALEEM commit the offence of obstructing a police officer (contrary to s. 89(2) of the Police Act 1996)?

A No, HALEEM must either intend to obstruct a police officer in the lawful execution of his/her duty or be reckless as to whether the officer will be obstructed.
B Yes, when HALEEM saw the officer struggling and did nothing to help.
C No, HALEEM did not wilfully obstruct PC BURN.
D Yes, when HALEEM made it harder for the officer to carry out the lawful execution of his duty.

103. EWER has an argument with BASSFORD (her next-door neighbour) regarding noise from a party that BASSFORD is holding in his back garden. BASSFORD has positioned two large speakers in his back garden and EWER says these are causing far too much noise. EWER decides that she will cut the wires leading to the speakers that BASSFORD has set up in his garden and she has just the thing to accomplish that in her garden shed—telescopic pruning shears. She walks towards her shed to pick up the shears but as she does so a power surge blows BASSFORD's speakers and stops the noise.

Does EWER commit an offence of possessing an article with intent to cause criminal damage (contrary to s. 3 of the Criminal Damage Act 1971)?

A Yes, when she decides to use the shears to cut the speaker wires.
B No, this activity is taking place in a private garden not a public place.
C Yes, but not until she begins to walk towards the garden shed.
D No, as she never picked up the shears, she never physically possessed them.

104. PC MADDOX is an advanced police driver on uniform patrol in a marked vehicle equipped with audible and visual warning systems ('blues and twos'). The officer is overtaken by a stolen Ford Mustang motor vehicle driven by PENNY. PC MADDOX turns on the 'blues and twos' and follows the Mustang. Both vehicles drive through a set of traffic lights at a cross junction showing red against them and consequently PC MADDOX is involved in a collision with a car driven by SHEPHERD (driving through the junction with the lights in his favour) and PC MADDOX is injured. As a result of the incident, consideration is being given to the possibility of charging PC MADDOX with an offence of dangerous driving (contrary to s. 2 of the Road Traffic Act 1988).

Which of the statements below is correct when considering the law and defences to dangerous driving that are relevant to PC MADDOX and PENNY's liability under civil law?

A Whilst the particular circumstances under which PC MADDOX was driving may not provide a specific defence, they may nevertheless provide mitigation and, where appropriate, special reasons for not disqualifying him.

B If charged with the offence, PC MADDOX would be entitled to have his ability as an advanced police driver with highly developed driving skills taken into account when deciding if the driving in question was dangerous.

C PC MADDOX would be able to utilise the defence of necessity in these circumstances.

D PENNY could not be sued for damages as a result of the injury to PC MADDOX.

105. PC OZDEMIR has arrested PEARCE in relation to an offence of robbery. The officer is putting together an interview plan which involves consideration of what information to make available to PEARCE's solicitor, CARTER. PC OZDEMIR approaches you, as her supervisor, for some advice regarding what should be disclosed to a solicitor prior to the interview with PEARCE. The officer is unsure about whether the custody record and an initial description given by a witness of the offender (the 'first description') should be disclosed.

Must both or either of these items be disclosed to CARTER before the interview with PEARCE takes place?

A Yes, the custody record and the record of 'first description' must be provided to CARTER before PEARCE is interviewed about the offence.

B No, there is no provision within the Police and Criminal Evidence Act 1984 or the Codes of Practice for the disclosure of any information by the police at the police station.

C Yes, the custody record must be disclosed.

D No, although if these items are not disclosed then no inference could be drawn by a court from PEARCE's silence.

106. DC JAMES (who is dressed in plain clothes) is making enquiries at a number of houses near to the scene of a burglary. He is invited into a house by a resident, Alan SMETHAM (aged 16 years), and moves through the hallway of the house into the lounge. At this time, Kurt SMETHAM (the father of Alan and the owner of the house) appears and tells DC JAMES that he is not welcome and that he should leave immediately. Alan SMETHAM tells the officer that if his father says that he should leave then that is exactly what the officer should do. As DC JAMES is leaving the house via the hallway, he notices a watch on a table by the front door. DC JAMES reasonably suspects that the watch is an item of property that was stolen in the burglary he is investigating.

Can DC JAMES use the powers under s. 19 of the Police and Criminal Evidence Act 1984 to seize the item of property?

A No, as the officer only reasonably suspects that the watch was stolen in the burglary.

B Yes, as DC JAMES was invited into the premises by a resident and that means he is lawfully on the premises.

C No, as DC JAMES is not 'lawfully' on the premises.

D Yes, as s. 19 provides a power of entry to all constables to search for stolen goods.

107. PC MONTIERO is on uniform mobile patrol when she is sent to a disturbance outside a council building. When the officer arrives, she is spoken to by WRAGG who tells the officer that a few moments before the officer arrived a group of people shouting and using extreme political language had been causing trouble outside the council building. One of them had dropped a bag outside the council building and told WRAGG that it contained an explosive. PC MONTIERO believes the situation is 'urgent' and is considering whether she can designate an area around the bag as a 'cordoned area' under ss. 33 to 36 of the Terrorism Act 2000.

Could PC MONTIERO make such a designation?

A No, such a designation can only be made by an officer of the rank of inspector or above.

B No, such a designation can only be made by an officer of the rank of assistant chief constable (or commander) or above.

C Yes, but it cannot be given orally, it must be in writing.

D Yes, and PC MONTIERO must ensure an officer of the rank of superintendent or above is informed of the designation.

108. Kelly SAMUELSON and Amy SAMUELSON are civil partners but have argued and decided to split up. The pair have since argued about who owns what in the house they shared before Kelly moved out three weeks ago. Kelly returns to the house with ORTEGA (her friend) while Amy is at work, with the idea of removing several items of property that Kelly says belong to her. Once inside the house, Kelly becomes upset and says to ORTEGA, *'I don't care about taking my things—smash them instead!'* Kelly and ORTEGA cause damage to a TV in the lounge of the house. The TV belongs to Kelly and also belongs to Amy as they purchased it jointly (a fact that Kelly is aware of). ORTEGA is unaware of this and believes the TV belongs solely to Kelly and that she wants the TV damaged.

Considering the offence of criminal damage (under s. 1(1) of the Criminal Damage Act 1971), which of the following comments is correct?

- **A** ORTEGA would be able to state that she had a 'lawful excuse' to damage the TV if she were charged with criminal damage; Kelly SAMUELSON could be charged with an offence of criminal damage but such a prosecution could only be instituted with the consent of the DPP.
- **B** ORTEGA has committed criminal damage and has no defence; Kelly SAMUELSON could not be charged with criminal damage as the property belongs to her.
- **C** As the property belongs to Kelly SAMUELSON, no offence of criminal damage has taken place in these circumstances.
- **D** Kelly SAMUELSON and ORTEGA could both be charged with criminal damage; the consent of the DPP is not required as the property damaged also belonged to Amy SAMUELSON.

109. RIBITSCH and BENTHAM meet at a party and in conversation they find out that they both have an interest in sadomasochistic sexual activities. They agree to meet at RIBITSCH's house where they will have sexual intercourse and engage in sadomasochistic activities where they will cause serious injury to each other for the purposes of obtaining sexual gratification. The pair meet at RIBITSCH's home the following day and they have sexual intercourse. During the sexual intercourse, BENTHAM tells RIBITSCH to punch him in the face; RIBITSCH does and causes BENTHAM to temporarily lose consciousness (a s. 47 Offences Against the Person Act 1861 offence). BENTHAM regains consciousness and tells RIBITSCH to hit him much harder; RIBITSCH does so and breaks BENTHAM's jaw (a s. 20 Offences Against the Person Act 1861 offence). RIBITSCH screams *'Do the same to me!'* and, intending to cause RIBITSCH serious injury, BENTHAM hits her in the face and breaks her jaw (a s. 18 Offences Against the Person Act 1861 offence).

At what stage, if at all, would the provisions of s. 71(2) of the Domestic Abuse Act 2021 (consenting to serious harm for the purposes of sexual gratification) first be relevant to the offence committed?

- **A** Section 71(2) would be irrelevant to this scenario.
- **B** When the s. 47 offence is committed.
- **C** When the s. 20 offence is committed.
- **D** When the s. 18 offence is committed.

110. WHYBROW travels all over England and Wales doing odd jobs for cash payments and travelling from place to place by hitching rides, usually in haulage vehicles that carry goods. He is contacted by DUDLEY who tells WHYBROW he has work for him in Newcastle and the job starts tomorrow. WHYBROW is 190 miles away in Stoke-on-Trent and tries to hitch a lift but is unsuccessful. Desperate to get to Newcastle, WHYBROW manages to force open the back door of a haulage vehicle at a motorway service station (WHYBROW overheard the driver stating that he was transporting goods to Newcastle) and waits in the back of the vehicle to travel to Newcastle. The driver returns to the vehicle and drives off. The vehicle has travelled 100 miles before the driver discovers WHYBROW in the rear of the vehicle.

Does WHYBROW commit an offence of obtaining services dishonestly (contrary to s. 11 of the Fraud Act 2006)?

A Yes, and as the offence is a 'conduct' crime; it is committed when WHYBROW gets into the haulage vehicle intending to travel to Newcastle.

B No, the offence requires a fraudulent act to be carried out—this has not occurred in this situation.

C Yes, and as the offence is a 'result' crime, the offence is committed once the vehicle drives off from the motorway service station.

D No, as WHYBROW is not obtaining a service (the haulage company does not provide rides to people).

111. BERTRAND attacks CHEUNG in a street and fractures CHEUNG's skull. CHEUNG is rushed to hospital where an examination of CHEUNG shows that the fractured skull has caused brain damage. The seriousness of CHEUNG's situation is compounded by the fact that it is discovered that he has a serious stomach ulcer. The brain damage keeps CHEUNG in a coma and prevents doctors from operating on the stomach ulcer. One month later, the ulcer bursts and causes CHEUNG to die.

Considering concepts associated with criminal conduct and in particular the 'chain of causation', is BERTRAND liable for the death of CHEUNG?

A No, because the untreated ulcer, not the fractured skull, was the cause of CHEUNG's death.

B Yes, CHEUNG's death was a direct consequence of the assault by BERTRAND and, as the chain of causation can never be broken, BERTRAND is liable for CHEUNG's death.

C No, because of the time delay between the discovery of the ulcer and CHEUNG's death.

D Yes, but for BERTRAND's attack on CHEUNG the ulcer could have been operated on and he would not have died.

112. BUCKFIELD is shopping in a retail park and buys several packs of needles from a craft shop. BUCKFIELD intends to insert the needles into some apples he has at his home address and place the apples in a supermarket to cause public alarm and anxiety. He returns to his home and inserts needles into a dozen apples. He puts the contaminated apples into a bag and takes them to a supermarket near to his home; the supermarket sells various goods including apples. He enters the supermarket and is looking for an opportunity to place the apples down without being seen. He is standing in a deserted aisle stocked with computer games and, seeing his opportunity, he places the apples next to a display of computer games.

Considering the offence of contaminating or interfering with goods (contrary to s. 38(1) of the Public Order Act 1986), which of the following comments is correct?

A BUCKFIELD commits an offence when he purchases the needles to contaminate the apples.

B When BUCKFIELD contaminates the apples with needles at his home address, he commits no offence (because he is at his place of abode at that time).

C BUCKFIELD did not commit an offence when he placed the contaminated apples in the computer games aisle (that is not a place where goods of that description are sold).

D BUCKFIELD commits an offence as he has contaminated 'natural' goods (the apples); the offence would not be committed if the contaminated goods were 'manufactured'.

113. PC BARROWCLOUGH receives information that stolen property is being stored in three separate houses all owned by HIPGRAVE. The officer applies to a justice of the peace for a search warrant under s. 8 of the Police and Criminal Evidence Act 1984 to search the three premises and is granted a 'specific premises warrant' to search the three houses. The warrant authorises an unlimited number of entries to the premises.

According to s. 15 of the Police and Criminal Evidence Act 1984, how many copies of such a warrant will be made?

A One copy will be made of the warrant.

B Two copies will be made of the warrant.

C A copy will be made for every separate premises to be entered (in this case, that will be three copies).

D As many copies as are reasonably required may be made of the warrant.

114. CALDERDALE and KELT break into a house intending to steal property. CALDERDALE has a bayonet with him in his jacket pocket to stab anyone who gets in his way and KELT knows the bayonet is there as CALDERDALE told him he was bringing it with him. KELT has brought a small length of rope with him to tie up anyone who might cause them problems whilst they commit the offence, however he did not mention the fact that he had brought the rope with him to CALDERDALE.

Who, if anyone, commits an offence of aggravated burglary (contrary to s. 10 of the Theft Act 1968)?

A CALDERDALE and KELT in relation to the bayonet and KELT alone in relation to the rope.
B CALDERDALE and KELT in relation to the bayonet, neither in relation to the rope.
C CALDERDALE and KELT in relation to the bayonet and the rope.
D No offence of aggravated burglary has been committed in these circumstances.

115. DC KINGSTON receives reliable information from a covert human intelligence source (CHIS) that drugs are being stored at a warehouse on a small industrial estate. An operation is commenced in relation to the premises and a warrant (under s. 23 of the Misuse of Drugs Act 1971) is obtained to search the premises and persons within. When the warrant is executed, MILFORD (the owner of the warehouse) is found in an office inside the warehouse in possession of £20,000 worth of cocaine and £50,000 in cash. During the search, the police recover drugs paraphernalia (clingfilm and contact details of drug dealers) from the office. MILFORD is later charged with an offence of possession with intent to supply (contrary to s. 5(3) of the Misuse of Drugs Act 1971).

In relation to proving an intention to supply and potential defences to this offence, which of the following comments is correct?

A Possession of drugs paraphernalia will be evidence that proves the intention to supply.
B In proving an intention to supply, the prosecution would be able to cite as evidence the presence of the £50,000 cash found with the seized drugs.
C MILFORD would be able to utilise the defence under s. 5(4) of the Misuse of Drugs Act 1971 in respect of a charge of possession with intent to supply.
D MILFORD would not be able to utilise the general defence under s. 28 of the Misuse of Drugs Act 1971 Act in respect of a charge of possession with intent to supply.

116. In the early hours of the morning, GRAYSON and his wife are asleep in an upstairs bedroom of their house when they are woken by a noise from the downstairs lounge. GRAYSON is petrified that this is a burglar and grabs hold of the first thing to hand, in this case a golf club, to protect himself and his wife. Moments later, TINKLER bursts into the bedroom. Only thinking about protecting his wife, GRAYSON lashes out towards TINKLER with the golf club. The club strikes TINKLER on the shoulder and he falls to the floor. TINKLER shouts out, *'You'll pay for that, pal!'* and starts to get up, at which point GRAYSON, honestly believing it is necessary to do so, strikes TINKLER on the head with the golf club. This causes TINKLER severe injury leading to him being in a permanent vegetative state.

Would GRAYSON's use of force be considered legitimate in these circumstances?

A Yes, the use of even grossly disproportionate force can be justified in 'householder' cases.

B No, as GRAYSON was acting to protect his wife and not himself.

C Yes, the use of disproportionate force can be regarded as reasonable in 'householder' cases.

D No, as the use of disproportionate force cannot be justified in any circumstances.

117. LITTLE has been arrested for an offence of theft. He was taken to a designated police station where his detention was authorised by the custody officer (PS PAYNE) at 08.56hrs. Inspector DRUMMOND carried out LITTLE's first review at 14.00hrs that day.

Considering the issues dealt with by s. 40 of the Police and Criminal Evidence Act 1984 (dealing with reviews), which of the following comments is true?

A LITTLE's second review shall not be later than six hours after the first review (20.00hrs).

B LITTLE's second review shall not be later than nine hours after the first review (23.00hrs).

C LITTLE's second review shall not be later than 12 hours after detention was first authorised (20.56hrs).

D LITTLE's second review shall not be later than 15 hours after detention was first authorised (23.56hrs).

118. FORRESTER (aged 18 years) has been arrested for an offence of burglary at a sports equipment warehouse. The police have a large amount of evidence that strongly implicates FORRESTER in 25 other burglary offences which have all taken place in residential premises. DC McCOOK is the officer in charge of the case and he speaks to his supervisor, DS GOWLAND-WYNN, regarding FORRESTER and the burglaries. DS GOWLAND-WYNN suggests that when FORRESTER is charged with the burglary of the sports equipment warehouse, an application should be made to the magistrates' court to remand FORRESTER in police custody (under s. 128 of the Magistrates' Courts Act 1980) for the purpose of enquiring into offences.

In relation to such a remand in police custody, which of the following comments is correct?

A If such a remand is granted, it will enable DC McCOOK to make enquiries into all of the burglary offences (including the burglary of the sports equipment warehouse).

B FORRESTER can be remanded in police custody for a period not exceeding two clear days.

C FORRESTER cannot be remanded in custody as he is 18 years old (the power for a magistrates' court to remand a person in police custody only applies to a person who is over 21 years old).

D If FORRESTER is remanded in police custody, the conditions of his detention and periodic review will apply as if he were arrested without warrant on suspicion of having committed an offence.

119. Police officers visit the home address of INGON and arrest him on suspicion of committing an offence of child abduction (contrary to s. 2 of the Child Abduction Act 1984). Whilst INGON remains on the premises, the officers search his home address and in the process recover a rifle which fires 7.62 mm bullets and an imitation revolver.

In respect of the offence of possessing a firearm while committing or being arrested for a sch. 1 offence (contrary to s. 17(2) of the Firearms Act 1968), which of the following statements is correct?

A INGON commits the offence but this would only be in connection with the rifle.

B The offence is not committed as child abduction is not a sch. 1 offence.

C The offence is committed in respect of the rifle and the imitation firearm.

D INGON can only be found guilty of the s. 17(2) Firearms Act offence if he is found guilty of the child abduction offence first.

120. DYKE has been arrested in connection with an offence of driving a motor vehicle while over the prescribed limit (contrary to s. 5(1)(a) of the Road Traffic Act 1988). DYKE was required to provide evidential specimens of breath at a police station, both of which were over the prescribed alcohol limit. DYKE has been charged with the offence.

Could DYKE be detained at the police station using the power under s. 10 of the Road Traffic Act 1988 (detention of person affected)?

A Yes, if a constable has reasonable grounds for suspecting that were DYKE to drive a motor vehicle on a road he would commit an offence under s. 5 or 5A of the Road Traffic Act 1988.

B No, not unless a constable has consulted a medical practitioner regarding DYKE's ability to drive and that practitioner states that DYKE's ability to drive would be impaired.

C Yes, if a constable has reasonable grounds for believing that were DYKE to drive a mechanically propelled vehicle on a road he would commit an offence under s. 4, 5 or 5A of the Road Traffic Act 1988.

D No, as DYKE has not been arrested and charged with an offence under s. 5A of the Road Traffic Act 1988 (driving, attempting to drive or being in charge of a motor vehicle with a concentration of a specified drug above a specified limit).

121. VIVIER is holding a party at his house and has drunk a bottle of gin and is drunk. He decides to set out an obstacle course in his large, private rear garden and challenges his party guests to drive a 'Go-Ped' (a motorised scooter) as fast as they can through the obstacles. Several party guests drive through the course before VIVIER takes his turn. VIVIER is determined to win and accelerates the Go-Ped to its maximum speed (22 mph), but as he is going through one of the obstacles a 5-year-old child of one of the party guests runs out in front of him. As VIVIER is drunk, his reactions are slow and he cannot avoid the child and hits the child causing serious head injuries to the child in the process. The child is rushed to hospital but later dies as a consequence of the serious head injuries.

Could VIVIER be convicted of an offence of causing death by dangerous driving (contrary to s. 1 of the Road Traffic Act 1988) in these circumstances?

A Yes, and the fact that VIVIER was adversely affected by alcohol is, in itself, determinative to prove the offence.

B No, he was driving a mechanically propelled vehicle not a motor vehicle.

C Yes, and evidence of drink will be admissible where the quantity of it may have adversely affected the quality of VIVIER's driving.

D No, as the accident took place on private land rather than a road or public place.

122. PC GOLD (a probationary officer) is the first officer at the scene of a kidnapping offence. Several of his more senior (in terms of experience) colleagues also attend the incident and there is a discussion in relation to the circumstances of the offence. PC GOLD is confused by what his colleagues have said and is unsure of the law relating to the offence of kidnap so he approaches his supervisor for some advice regarding the offence.

In relation to the offence of kidnap (under common law), which of the comments by officers at the scene of the offence shows a correct understanding of the law?

A PC JOHNSON stated that causing a person to move from place to place when unaccompanied by the defendant would not constitute an offence of kidnap.

B PC ANWAR stated that a person must be taken or carried away by force if the offence is to be committed.

C PC YOUNG stated that if a person is moved only a short distance, the offence will not be made out.

D PC SMETHEM stated that the offence of kidnap cannot be 'attempted'.

123. An authorisation for officers to utilise the powers of stop and search in a specific location (under s. 47A of the Terrorism Act 2000) has been given. PC BUCHANAN is on uniform mobile patrol in the area where the authorisation is active and is following a vehicle driven by SNOOKS. PC BUCHANAN decides to stop and search the vehicle and SNOOKS for the purpose of discovering whether there is anything which may constitute evidence that the vehicle is being used for the purposes of terrorism or if SNOOKS is a terrorist. During the course of the search, PC BUCHANAN forms the reasonable suspicion that SNOOKS is a terrorist and arrests SNOOKS on that basis under s. 41 of the Terrorism Act 2000.

In relation to the behaviour of the officer, which of the following comments is correct?

A PC BUCHANAN correctly stopped the vehicle but has unlawfully arrested SNOOKS.

B PC BUCHANAN correctly stopped the vehicle and the arrest of SNOOKS was lawful.

C PC BUCHANAN could not stop the vehicle under s. 47A of the Terrorism Act 2000 (the officer should have used the general power to stop a vehicle under s. 163 of the Road Traffic Act 1988 and then searched SNOOKS).

D PC BUCHANAN could not stop the vehicle under s. 47A of the Terrorism Act 2000 unless he reasonably believed that the vehicle was being used for terrorist purposes.

124. BARTON is sitting in the lounge of his house with several friends—they are all watching an international rugby match between England and Scotland. It is a very hot day so he has the windows of the lounge open. During the match, the Scottish team score a try causing BARTON to scream in rage as he is supporting England. He uses extremely abusive language about the Scottish team and in doing so he intends to stir up racial hatred against the Scottish. As the windows in the lounge are open, this abusive language is heard by LEISHMAN who is BARTON's neighbour and is Scottish. LEISHMAN contacts the police to complain about BARTON's language. The language was not heard by anyone else.

In relation to the offence under s. 18 of the Public Order Act 1986 (use of words, behaviour or display of written material), which of the following comments is correct?

A The offence has been committed but only in relation to LEISHMAN (as he was not inside the same dwelling as BARTON).

B The offence has not been committed as it cannot be committed by a person who is inside a dwelling.

C The offence has been committed in relation to BARTON's friends inside the lounge of his house and also in relation to LEISHMAN.

D The offence is not committed as the language used by BARTON was not heard by anyone except for people in the same dwelling as BARTON or in another dwelling (LEISHMAN).

125. DC FISHLOCK (who is dressed in plain clothes) is driving an unmarked police vehicle along a road. Suddenly, a Fiat 500 motor vehicle being driven in front of DC FISHLOCK swerves and collides with a lamp post at the side of the road, damaging the Fiat 500 and the lamp post in the process. The officer stops, gets out of his vehicle, identifies himself as a police officer and speaks to BRADLEY who is the driver and only occupant of the Fiat 500 motor vehicle. Fortunately, BRADLEY is not injured. BRADLEY tells the officer that a dog ran out in front of his vehicle causing him to take avoiding action. Other than being slightly shaken up, BRADLEY appears to be fine and the officer does not suspect that he is under the influence of drink or drugs.

Can DC FISHLOCK require BRADLEY to take part in a preliminary test (under s. 6 of the Road Traffic Act 1988)?

A No, as the officer is not in uniform.

B Yes, and in addition DC FISHLOCK could administer the test.

C No, because the officer does not suspect that a person has been injured as a consequence of the accident.

D Yes, but the officer could not administer the test.

126. MEPSTEAD is applying for a mortgage to purchase his first house. He earns £37,000 a year but realises that this will not be quite enough to obtain the mortgage he requires to purchase the house so falsifies information in the mortgage application and makes it appear that he is earning £45,000 a year. He submits the mortgage application to his bank which later discovers that MEPSTEAD has lied on the mortgage application.

In relation to the offence of false accounting (contrary to s. 17 of the Theft Act 1968), which of the comments below is correct?

A No offence has been committed as the dishonest mortgage application was discovered and there was no 'gain or loss in money or other property' as a result.

B The offence has been committed by MEPSTEAD as a mortgage application has been held to be a document required for an accounting purpose.

C No offence has been committed as MEPSTEAD did not destroy, deface or conceal any account required for an accounting purpose.

D The offence has been committed but in order to prove the offence the prosecution will be required to prove an intention to permanently deprive by MEPSTEAD.

127. A number of public order incidents have occurred outside a house owned by COSTELLO due to a rumour that he has had a lottery win in excess of £50 million—this is not true. However, the rumour is being repeated on social media and the police are concerned that this will result in significant amounts of anti-social behaviour taking place outside COSTELLO's house. Consideration is being given to authorising the use of the dispersal power under part 3 of the Anti-social Behaviour, Crime and Policing Act 2014 in order to remove or reduce the likelihood of anti-social behaviour occurring.

In relation to such an authorisation and the powers that are associated with it, which of the following comments is correct?

A If a person is directed to leave under such an authorisation, that direction must be given in writing to ensure that the person is clear where they are being dispersed from.

B A person directed to leave a specified area subject to the authorisation can be directed not to return for a specified period of up to 72 hours.

C If authorised, the dispersal power is available to constables in uniform; it is not available to police community support officers.

D The authorisation can only be given where a police officer of or above the rank of inspector reasonably believes the exercise of the power is required.

128. WHYTE and SCOTT are walking towards JOHNSON'S house. SCOTT's mobile phone rings and SCOTT has a brief conversation and hangs up. SCOTT tells WHYTE that he has to go to his mother's house and cannot accompany WHYTE to JOHNSON's house. SCOTT passes WHYTE a small envelope and asks WHYTE to give this to JOHNSON as JOHNSON is expecting it. WHYTE asks what is in the envelope and SCOTT replies '£200 cash'. WHYTE has no reason to disbelieve SCOTT and tells him that he will deliver the money to JOHNSON. WHYTE continues his journey and on the way to JOHNSON's house he is stopped by a police officer. The police officer searches WHYTE and finds the envelope. When the officer opens the envelope, it is found to contain an amount of cocaine and not £200 cash as WHYTE had been informed.

Is WHYTE in 'possession' of the cocaine?

A Yes, as he has physical control over it as well as knowledge of its presence.
B No, as although he knew he had possession of the envelope he did not know that it contained cocaine.
C Yes, as all that is required to prove 'possession' is that a person has physical control over something.
D No, as he thought there was £200 cash inside the envelope.

129. SETTELIN has been arrested for an offence of attempted murder and is in custody at a designated police station. The custody officer, PS DREW, asks SETTELIN if he wants anyone informed of his whereabouts and SETTELIN responds by saying that he would like WILSON to be told. The arresting officer, DC FRANCIS, has information that suggests WILSON was involved in the offence and objects to WILSON being informed of SETTELIN's whereabouts as it will alert WILSON to the fact that he is wanted for the offence.

In relation to delaying SETTELIN's right to have someone informed of his whereabouts, which of the following comments is correct?

A An officer of the rank of inspector or above can authorise the delay which cannot be delayed beyond 24 hours after the relevant time.
B An officer of the rank of superintendent or above can authorise the delay which cannot be delayed beyond 24 hours after the relevant time.
C An officer of the rank of inspector or above can authorise the delay which cannot be delayed beyond 36 hours after the relevant time.
D An officer of the rank of superintendent or above can authorise the delay which cannot be delayed beyond 36 hours after the relevant time.

130. A large number of burglaries at commercial premises have taken place and goods to the value of £2 million pounds have been stolen. An operation is commenced in relation to the offences leading to the arrest of CALDERDALE who is later charged with the burglary offences. Sergeant WARWICK is the disclosure officer in the case and is liaising with his Professional Standards Department as to whether information regarding allegations of, and the misconduct of, several officers involved in the investigation should be revealed to the prosecutor.

Considering the Disclosure Code of Practice and advice given to prosecutors by the Director of Public Prosecutions, which of the following comments is correct?

A Sergeant WARWICK will have the final responsibility for the value judgement on whether information relating to misconduct of police officers should be revealed to the prosecutor.

B Findings in relation to disciplinary matters, regardless of their nature, must always be revealed to the prosecution who must, in turn, disclose them to the defence.

C There is no duty on the prosecution to disclose details of unsubstantiated complaints against a police officer.

D Disciplinary matters are not criminal convictions and consequently have no relevance as far as disclosure is concerned.

131. CUNLIFFE moves into a house directly opposite one owned by MORRITT. CUNLIFFE holds a series of noisy parties over several weeks resulting in MORRITT complaining about the noise and the police visiting CUNLIFFE's house. CUNLIFFE decides that he will cause serious problems for MORRITT and burn his house down. To do so, he makes a petrol bomb (using petrol, a milk bottle and an old rag). He waits until MORRITT's house is empty and walks over to the house. Outside the house, he lights the petrol bomb and throws it at MORRITT's house. As he does this, the rag falls out of the petrol bomb and the bottle hits the house, failing to ignite.

At what stage, if at all, does CUNLIFFE attempt to commit an offence of arson (under s. 1 of the Criminal Attempts Act 1981)?

A When he makes the petrol bomb.

B When he walks over to MORRITT's house.

C When he throws the petrol bomb at the house.

D The offence is not committed because the petrol bomb did not ignite.

132. William ABBOTT has been arrested on suspicion of committing an offence of murder. At the time of the offence, Felicity ABBOTT (the wife of William ABBOTT) was with her husband and although she had no involvement in the offence she did see exactly what happened. While William ABBOTT is in custody awaiting interview, DC PARRIS (who is part of the investigation team) is gathering evidence and interviews Felicity ABBOTT about the incident. DC PARRIS obtains a witness statement from Felicity ABBOTT describing what she saw occur. William ABBOTT is charged with the murder offence and pleads 'not guilty'.

Considering the law in respect of the compellability of Felicity ABBOTT to give evidence for the prosecution, which of the following statements is correct?

A The statement from Felicity ABBOTT could be admitted in evidence even if she refused to give evidence against her husband.
B Felicity ABBOTT is not compellable to give evidence against her husband in this matter and DC PARRIS should have informed her of this before taking any statement; the statement obtained could not be admitted in evidence.
C Murder is a 'specified offence' under s. 80(2A) of the Police and Criminal Evidence Act 1984, meaning that Felicity ABBOTT is compellable to give evidence for the prosecution.
D A wife cannot be compelled to give evidence against her husband regardless of the crime the husband is accused of.

133. ROUGHTON has found out that CRANE (his girlfriend) has been having an affair with his best friend. ROUGHTON and CRANE live together in rented accommodation and have been saving for a deposit for a house. Out of a desire for revenge, ROUGHTON grabs a large tin of paint and pours it over £2,000 in cash that they had hidden in a drawer in the bedroom of the house. ROUGHTON then takes a pair of scissors and cuts up three designer shirts that CRANE had given to him as a birthday present.

Has ROUGHTON committed an offence of criminal damage (contrary to s. 1(1) of the Criminal Damage Act 1971) in this situation?

A Yes, to the money and the shirts.
B No, money is not 'property' for the purposes of the Criminal Damage Act 1971 and you cannot cause criminal damage to property that you own (the shirts).
C Yes, to the money alone.
D No, the money and the shirts belong to ROUGHTON.

134. CRUIKSHANK has been arrested for an offence of violent disorder and is being interviewed about the offence at a designated police station—the interview is being visually recorded. CRUIKSHANK is legally represented in the interview by his solicitor. The interviewing officers ask a number of questions of CRUIKSHANK during the interview but he remains completely silent having been told to do so by his solicitor who has told the interviewing officers that he has advised his client to do so in response to all questions put to him in interview. CRUIKSHANK genuinely relies on the advice of his solicitor to remain silent.

Could adverse inferences (under s. 34 of the Criminal Justice and Public Order Act 1994) be drawn from CRUIKSHANK's failure to respond to questions in the interview?

A No, CRUIKSHANK's genuine reliance on the advice of his solicitor to stay silent is not, in itself, enough to preclude adverse inferences.

B Yes, CRUIKSHANK could be convicted solely on an inference drawn from silence.

C No, adverse inferences can only be drawn from an interview where the defendant responds to questioning; they cannot be drawn from an interview where the defendant remains silent.

D Yes, adverse inferences may be drawn from CRUIKSHANK's silence but only because he was legally represented during the course of the interview.

135. PC BRIDIE has arrested CHUNTAO for an offence of burglary and has taken him to a designated police station. PC BRIDIE wants to search a flat which is owned by CHUNTAO for evidence in connection with the burglary CHUNTAO has been arrested for.

Which of the following comments is correct in relation to the use of the power under s. 18 of the Police and Criminal Evidence Act 1984 in this situation?

A PC BRIDIE must have reasonable grounds to suspect that there is evidence on the premises relating to the burglary or some other indictable offence which is connected to the burglary or similar to it. If that is the case, an officer of the rank of inspector or above could provide an oral authorisation for the use of the s. 18 power.

B PC BRIDIE must have reasonable grounds to believe that there is evidence on the premises relating to the burglary or some other indictable offence which is connected to the burglary or similar to it. If that is the case, an officer of the rank of inspector or above could provide a written authorisation for the use of the s. 18 power.

C PC BRIDIE must have reasonable grounds to believe that there is evidence on the premises relating to the burglary or some other indictable offence which is connected to the burglary or similar to it. If that is the case, an officer of the rank of inspector or above could provide an oral authorisation for the use of the s. 18 power.

D PC BRIDIE must have reasonable grounds to suspect that there is evidence on the premises relating to the burglary or some other indictable offence which is connected to the burglary or similar to it. If that is the case, an officer of the rank of inspector or above could provide a written authorisation for the use of the s. 18 power.

136. HUTTON and TAGG are standing on a street outside the offices of International Care Ltd and protesting against the activities of the company as they believe the company is involved in animal experiments. HUTTON and TAGG have been speaking to employees of the company as they enter the premises and trying to persuade them not to go into work. PC FITZPATRICK (on uniform patrol) is sent to the incident and, after speaking to HUTTON and TAGG, he forms the opinion that the presence of HUTTON and TAGG at the scene is likely to cause alarm or distress to the employees of International Care Ltd.

Could PC FITZPATRICK use the powers under s. 42 of the Criminal Justice and Police Act 2001 to direct HUTTON and TAGG to leave the vicinity?

A No, because s. 42 powers are only available to prevent the intimidation or harassment of people in their own or others' homes.

B Yes, but only because the officer is in uniform.

C No, because a direction to leave the vicinity under s. 42 can only be given by an officer of the rank of inspector or above.

D Yes, and the direction will require HUTTON and TAGG to leave the vicinity and not to return to it within such a period as PC FITZPATRICK may specify, not being for a period longer than three months.

137. HATTON and BRYDER are drinking in a pub when they become involved in a dispute about football. HATTON is annoyed at BRYDER and swings his fist at BRYDER intending to punch him in the face and injure him. HATTON does not intend to cause serious injury to BRYDER but does appreciate that if the blow lands then it will cause some harm to BRYDER. BRYDER sees the blow coming and, believing he is going to be harmed, he ducks and HATTON misses him. However, HATTON's momentum carries him forward and the punch aimed at BRYDER strikes OGDEN (who was standing behind BRYDER) in the face. The blow to OGDEN's face breaks OGDEN's jaw.

Considering offences relating to attempts, assault and the doctrine of transferred *mens rea*, which of the following comments is correct?

A HATTON has committed an offence of s. 39 assault (contrary to the Criminal Justice Act 1988) against BRYDER and an offence of s. 20 grievous bodily harm (contrary to the Offences Against the Person Act 1861) against OGDEN.

B HATTON has committed an offence of attempted battery (contrary to s. 1 of the Criminal Attempts Act 1981) against BRYDER and an offence of s. 20 grievous bodily harm (contrary to the Offences Against the Person Act 1861) against OGDEN.

C HATTON has committed an offence of s. 39 assault (contrary to the Criminal Justice Act 1988) against BRYDER and an offence of s. 18 grievous bodily harm (contrary to the Offences Against the Person Act 1861) against OGDEN.

D HATTON has committed an offence of s. 39 assault (contrary to the Criminal Justice Act 1988) against BRYDER but is not liable for any offence in relation to the injury caused to OGDEN.

138. PC KERSLAKE (who is on uniform mobile patrol) has attended the scene of an accident where two motor vehicles collided with each other. The officer required the drivers of both vehicles to take part in a preliminary breath test; PENNY (the driver of one of the vehicles) failed that test.

With regard to the requirement for an evidential breath specimen from PENNY (under s. 7 of the Road Traffic Act 1988), which of the following statements is correct?

A PC KERSLAKE could only make this requirement at a police station.

B PC KERSLAKE could only make this requirement at a police station or at a hospital.

C PC KERSLAKE could make this requirement at a police station, a hospital or other medical premises.

D PC KERSLAKE can make the requirement at or near the place where the preliminary breath test has been administered to PENNY.

139. ANDERSON is outside a shopping centre and is behaving in a very strange way, so much so that the police have been called as there are concerns about ANDERSON. PCs GOATLEY and YOUNG arrive and speak to ANDERSON who shouts at the officers, *'You are all agents of the evil one and I shall destroy you with my wand of fire!'* whilst waving a wooden stick at the officers. It appears to the officers that ANDERSON is suffering from a mental disorder and is in immediate need of care and control so they detain him under s. 136 of the Mental Health Act 1983.

In relation to the power under s. 136 of the Act, which of the following comments is correct?

A ANDERSON should be taken to a place of safety but under no circumstances should this be a police station.

B The decision to use a police station as a place of safety must be authorised by an officer of the rank of inspector or above.

C The maximum time a person removed to a place of safety can be detained for cannot exceed 72 hours.

D If ANDERSON is taken to a place of safety by the police, he will be considered to be in 'police detention'.

140. O'BRIEN has been arrested for a series of high-profile murders and taken to a designated police station to be questioned regarding the offences. Due to the complex and detailed nature of the offences alleged to have been committed by O'BRIEN, the interview team responsible for questioning him are considering how long they will have to deal with him and discuss a superintendent's custody time extension and also warrants of further detention from a magistrates' court.

Using all of those extensions, what is the maximum period that O'BRIEN can be kept in custody without being charged?

A 60 hours.

B 72 hours.

C 84 hours.

D 96 hours.

141. PC CULPAN (a female officer) and PC KHAN (a male officer) stop FRASER in a public place and search him under s. 23 of the Misuse of Drugs Act 1971. During the search, PC CULPAN places her hands inside the pockets of a coat FRASER is wearing. Nothing is found during a cursory search but the officers decide a more thorough search is required and they take FRASER into a police van (the inside of which cannot be seen by the public). Inside the van, PC KHAN requires FRASER to remove his headwear and then PC CULPAN requires FRASER to remove his shoes. The officers find nothing during the course of the search—they make a record of the search and FRASER leaves.

Which of the following statements is correct?

A PC CULPAN should not have placed her hands into FRASER's coat.

B The search could have taken place at a police station or other location out of public view but not a police vehicle.

C PC CULPAN should not have been present in the police vehicle when FRASER was required to remove his headgear.

D There was nothing wrong with PC CULPAN asking FRASER to remove his shoes.

142. LAVENDER has been arrested on suspicion of possessing a controlled drug with intent to supply (contrary to s. 5(3) of the Misuse of Drugs Act 1971) and is in police detention. The controlled drug in question is cannabis resin (a Class B drug). The arresting officer, DC ADAMS, has informed the custody officer, PS GOODINSON, that she saw LAVENDER swallow something just prior to his arrest and believes this may be some of the controlled drug (cannabis resin). DC ADAMS suggests to PS GOODINSON that it might be a good idea to carry out an X-ray or an ultrasound scan on LAVENDER.

Considering the power under s. 55A of the Police and Criminal Evidence Act 1984 to take X-rays or ultrasound scans, which of the following statements is correct?

A An X-ray or ultrasound scan could be taken of LAVENDER with the authorisation of the custody officer and the written consent of LAVENDER.

B An X-ray or ultrasound scan could not be taken in this situation as cannabis resin is not a Class A drug.

C An X-ray or ultrasound scan could be taken of LAVENDER with the written consent of an officer of the rank of inspector or above; force can be used to obtain the X-ray or ultrasound scan.

D An X-ray or ultra-sound scan could not be taken in this situation as the power is available only when someone has swallowed something that might be used to harm themselves or another.

143. RISTIC has been convicted of an offence of supplying a controlled drug (contrary to s. 4(3) of the Misuse of Drugs Act 1971) and sentenced to a term of imprisonment of three years for the offence.

Would the court have a duty to consider whether or not a travel restriction order would be appropriate in these circumstances?

A No, as supplying a controlled drug is not a 'drug trafficking offence'.
B Yes, and if the court imposed the travel restriction order it would last for a minimum period of three years.
C No, RISTIC has only been sentenced to three years' imprisonment not four or more.
D Yes, and once imposed the travel restriction order cannot be revoked or suspended.

144. Serious disorder takes place at a pub and several people are stabbed. Inspector BRANNAN authorises the use of the power under s. 60 of the Criminal Justice and Public Order Act 1994 in response to the incident. A significant number of police officers are at the scene including PC MAKIN (in uniform) and DC VERNEY (who is dressed in plain clothes). The two officers are chatting when FUREY walks by them wearing a baseball cap on his head and a scarf over his face so that only his eyes can be seen. Both officers reasonably believe FUREY is wearing the cap and scarf to conceal his identity.

Which of the following comments is correct?

A PC MAKIN or DC VERNEY could require FUREY to remove the baseball cap and scarf.
B Only PC MAKIN could require FUREY to remove the baseball cap and scarf.
C Neither officer could require the removal of the baseball cap and scarf.
D PC MAKIN or DC VERNEY could require FUREY to remove the baseball cap and scarf and also search FUREY for other items that could be used to conceal his identity.

145. LARIBA was arrested and interviewed regarding an offence of robbery. LARIBA states that he is innocent and disputes the identification evidence of an eye-witness to the offence and, consequently, the police have arranged an identification parade. LARIBA's solicitor, MYERS, has requested that he is present when the identification parade takes place.

In relation to the request by MYERS and the procedure dealing with video identification parades (in Annex A of Code D of the Codes of Practice), which of the comments below is correct?

A LARIBA may be present when the video identification procedure takes place if he requests to be present and with the prior agreement of the identification officer.
B During the identification procedure MYERS would not be allowed to communicate with the eye-witness or the identification officer.
C If the identification officer is satisfied that MYERS's presence will not deter or distract the eye-witness from viewing the images and making an identification, then he can be present when the video identification procedure takes place
D A supervised viewing of the recording of the video identification procedure by MYERS and/ or LARIBA may be arranged on request, at the discretion of the identification officer.

146. ROE is at a large rock concert which he and tens of thousands of others have paid to attend. One of the female singers at the concert performs her act wearing a very revealing outfit which ROE finds sexually stimulating. ROE leaves the main concert arena and goes into one of the single portable toilets on the concert site. In the privacy of the single toilet, he masturbates and ejaculates.

With regard to the offence of engaging in sexual activity in a public lavatory (contrary to s. 71 of the Sexual Offences Act 2003), which of the following statements is correct?

A ROE has committed the offence in these circumstances.

B The offence has not been committed as this is not a 'public' lavatory.

C The offence has not been committed as ROE cannot be seen by another member of the public.

D The offence has not been committed as ROE did not engage in sexual activity with another person.

147. PC GALLO has arrested TUCKWELL for an offence under s. 4(1) of the Road Traffic Act 1988 (driving whilst unfit through drink or drugs). At the police station, TUCKWELL provides two specimens of breath, both of which fall below 35 microgrammes of alcohol in 100 millilitres of breath. PC GALLO considers that TUCKWELL is 'high' on a drug and wishes TUCKWELL to supply a sample of blood or urine for analysis.

In these circumstances, can TUCKWELL be required to provide an evidential specimen of blood or urine (under s. 7 of the Road Traffic Act 1988)?

A Yes, but if TUCKWELL supplies a specimen of urine, it must be provided within two hours of the requirement for its provision being made and after the provision of a previous specimen of urine.

B No, as TUCKWELL has already provided two samples of breath, he has complied with the law and may not be requested to supply either a blood or urine sample.

C Yes, a blood or urine sample may only be obtained if PC GALLO has been advised by a medical practitioner that TUCKWELL's condition might be due to some drug.

D No, as a requirement for a specimen of blood or urine can only be made at a hospital.

148. BUSHNETT has been charged with an offence of assault (contrary to s. 47 of the Offences Against the Person Act 1861) and has been bailed by the police to make a first appearance at a magistrates' court in relation to the offence. BUSHNETT does not appear at court on that date and is later arrested for absconding (under s. 7 of the Bail Act 1976). When arrested, BUSHNETT states that he had a reasonable excuse for his failure to appear as he made a genuine error about his date of appearance at the magistrates' court; this came about because the police failed to give him a copy of the record of the decision to bail him (which included the date he was supposed to appear on).

In relation to the offence under s. 6 of the Bail Act 1976 (offence of absconding by a person released on bail), which of the following comments is correct?

A BUSHNETT has a 'reasonable excuse' for his failure to appear (the failure by the police to provide him with a copy of the record of the decision).

B The offence under s. 6 would not be appropriate as this is limited to a situation where the person fails to appear at a court having been granted bail by a court (not 'police bail').

C The facts that BUSHNETT made a genuine error about his date of appearance and that the police did not give him a copy of the record of the bail decision are irrelevant; he has committed the offence in these circumstances.

D BUSHNETT has a 'reasonable excuse' for his failure to appear (the fact that he made a genuine error about his date of appearance).

149. THOMAS has been arrested in connection with an offence of kidnapping. The victim of the kidnap, HUDSON, has not been found and there is great concern about her safety. There is sufficient evidence to provide a realistic prospect of conviction for the offence and consequently THOMAS is charged with kidnapping (contrary to common law). When THOMAS is charged with the offence and cautioned, he responds to the caution by saying, '*I want to tell you where she is.*'

Could THOMAS be interviewed about the offence of kidnapping at this stage?

A No, as THOMAS has been charged with the offence, he may not be interviewed any further in relation to it.

B Yes, as the interview would take place to prevent or minimise harm to some other person.

C No, as the person charged can only be further interviewed in order to clear up an ambiguity in a previous answer or statement.

D Yes, as long as an officer of the rank of superintendent or above authorises the interview to take place.

150. ISMAIL has been charged with an offence of burglary and the custody officer, PS CRAMPTON, is considering granting conditional bail to ISMAIL. One of the conditions that PS CRAMPTON is considering is that ISMAIL provides a surety in order that he surrenders to custody in the future.

In relation to the provision of a surety under s. 8 of the Bail Act 1976, which of the following comments is correct?

A PS CRAMPTON can impose the condition that ISMAIL will provide one surety—requiring ISMAIL to provide more than one surety is not permitted under the provisions of the Bail Act 1976.

B If a surety be identified and ISMAIL is granted bail but fails to surrender to custody, it will be necessary to prove that the surety had some involvement with ISMAIL's non-appearance in order for the cash or security involved to be forfeited.

C The imposition of a surety condition would require the authority of an officer of the rank of at least inspector.

D In considering the suitability of any proposed surety for ISMAIL, PS CRAMPTON may have regard to the proximity of the surety to ISMAIL (i.e. the place of residence of the surety).

Marking instructions

- Mark like this ⊨
- Make no stray marks
- Please do **NOT** tick, cross or circle

Answer Sheet

OXFORD
UNIVERSITY PRESS

Blackstone's Police Sergeants' and Inspectors' Mock Examination Paper 2023

1	�A ⊏B⊐ ⊏C⊐ ⊏D⊐	51	⊏A⊐ ⊏B⊐ ⊏C⊐ ⊏D⊐	101	⊏A⊐ ⊏B⊐ ⊏C⊐ ⊏D⊐
2	⊏A⊐ ⊏B⊐ ⊏C⊐ ⊏D⊐	52	⊏A⊐ ⊏B⊐ ⊏C⊐ ⊏D⊐	102	⊏A⊐ ⊏B⊐ ⊏C⊐ ⊏D⊐
3	⊏A⊐ ⊏B⊐ ⊏C⊐ ⊏D⊐	53	⊏A⊐ ⊏B⊐ ⊏C⊐ ⊏D⊐	103	⊏A⊐ ⊏B⊐ ⊏C⊐ ⊏D⊐
4	⊏A⊐ ⊏B⊐ ⊏C⊐ ⊏D⊐	54	⊏A⊐ ⊏B⊐ ⊏C⊐ ⊏D⊐	104	⊏A⊐ ⊏B⊐ ⊏C⊐ ⊏D⊐
5	⊏A⊐ ⊏B⊐ ⊏C⊐ ⊏D⊐	55	⊏A⊐ ⊏B⊐ ⊏C⊐ ⊏D⊐	105	⊏A⊐ ⊏B⊐ ⊏C⊐ ⊏D⊐
6	⊏A⊐ ⊏B⊐ ⊏C⊐ ⊏D⊐	56	⊏A⊐ ⊏B⊐ ⊏C⊐ ⊏D⊐	106	⊏A⊐ ⊏B⊐ ⊏C⊐ ⊏D⊐
7	⊏A⊐ ⊏B⊐ ⊏C⊐ ⊏D⊐	57	⊏A⊐ ⊏B⊐ ⊏C⊐ ⊏D⊐	107	⊏A⊐ ⊏B⊐ ⊏C⊐ ⊏D⊐
8	⊏A⊐ ⊏B⊐ ⊏C⊐ ⊏D⊐	58	⊏A⊐ ⊏B⊐ ⊏C⊐ ⊏D⊐	108	⊏A⊐ ⊏B⊐ ⊏C⊐ ⊏D⊐
9	⊏A⊐ ⊏B⊐ ⊏C⊐ ⊏D⊐	59	⊏A⊐ ⊏B⊐ ⊏C⊐ ⊏D⊐	109	⊏A⊐ ⊏B⊐ ⊏C⊐ ⊏D⊐
10	⊏A⊐ ⊏B⊐ ⊏C⊐ ⊏D⊐	60	⊏A⊐ ⊏B⊐ ⊏C⊐ ⊏D⊐	110	⊏A⊐ ⊏B⊐ ⊏C⊐ ⊏D⊐
11	⊏A⊐ ⊏B⊐ ⊏C⊐ ⊏D⊐	61	⊏A⊐ ⊏B⊐ ⊏C⊐ ⊏D⊐	111	⊏A⊐ ⊏B⊐ ⊏C⊐ ⊏D⊐
12	⊏A⊐ ⊏B⊐ ⊏C⊐ ⊏D⊐	62	⊏A⊐ ⊏B⊐ ⊏C⊐ ⊏D⊐	112	⊏A⊐ ⊏B⊐ ⊏C⊐ ⊏D⊐
13	⊏A⊐ ⊏B⊐ ⊏C⊐ ⊏D⊐	63	⊏A⊐ ⊏B⊐ ⊏C⊐ ⊏D⊐	113	⊏A⊐ ⊏B⊐ ⊏C⊐ ⊏D⊐
14	⊏A⊐ ⊏B⊐ ⊏C⊐ ⊏D⊐	64	⊏A⊐ ⊏B⊐ ⊏C⊐ ⊏D⊐	114	⊏A⊐ ⊏B⊐ ⊏C⊐ ⊏D⊐
15	⊏A⊐ ⊏B⊐ ⊏C⊐ ⊏D⊐	65	⊏A⊐ ⊏B⊐ ⊏C⊐ ⊏D⊐	115	⊏A⊐ ⊏B⊐ ⊏C⊐ ⊏D⊐
16	⊏A⊐ ⊏B⊐ ⊏C⊐ ⊏D⊐	66	⊏A⊐ ⊏B⊐ ⊏C⊐ ⊏D⊐	116	⊏A⊐ ⊏B⊐ ⊏C⊐ ⊏D⊐
17	⊏A⊐ ⊏B⊐ ⊏C⊐ ⊏D⊐	67	⊏A⊐ ⊏B⊐ ⊏C⊐ ⊏D⊐	117	⊏A⊐ ⊏B⊐ ⊏C⊐ ⊏D⊐
18	⊏A⊐ ⊏B⊐ ⊏C⊐ ⊏D⊐	68	⊏A⊐ ⊏B⊐ ⊏C⊐ ⊏D⊐	118	⊏A⊐ ⊏B⊐ ⊏C⊐ ⊏D⊐
19	⊏A⊐ ⊏B⊐ ⊏C⊐ ⊏D⊐	69	⊏A⊐ ⊏B⊐ ⊏C⊐ ⊏D⊐	119	⊏A⊐ ⊏B⊐ ⊏C⊐ ⊏D⊐
20	⊏A⊐ ⊏B⊐ ⊏C⊐ ⊏D⊐	70	⊏A⊐ ⊏B⊐ ⊏C⊐ ⊏D⊐	120	⊏A⊐ ⊏B⊐ ⊏C⊐ ⊏D⊐
21	⊏A⊐ ⊏B⊐ ⊏C⊐ ⊏D⊐	71	⊏A⊐ ⊏B⊐ ⊏C⊐ ⊏D⊐	121	⊏A⊐ ⊏B⊐ ⊏C⊐ ⊏D⊐
22	⊏A⊐ ⊏B⊐ ⊏C⊐ ⊏D⊐	72	⊏A⊐ ⊏B⊐ ⊏C⊐ ⊏D⊐	122	⊏A⊐ ⊏B⊐ ⊏C⊐ ⊏D⊐
23	⊏A⊐ ⊏B⊐ ⊏C⊐ ⊏D⊐	73	⊏A⊐ ⊏B⊐ ⊏C⊐ ⊏D⊐	123	⊏A⊐ ⊏B⊐ ⊏C⊐ ⊏D⊐
24	⊏A⊐ ⊏B⊐ ⊏C⊐ ⊏D⊐	74	⊏A⊐ ⊏B⊐ ⊏C⊐ ⊏D⊐	124	⊏A⊐ ⊏B⊐ ⊏C⊐ ⊏D⊐
25	⊏A⊐ ⊏B⊐ ⊏C⊐ ⊏D⊐	75	⊏A⊐ ⊏B⊐ ⊏C⊐ ⊏D⊐	125	⊏A⊐ ⊏B⊐ ⊏C⊐ ⊏D⊐
26	⊏A⊐ ⊏B⊐ ⊏C⊐ ⊏D⊐	76	⊏A⊐ ⊏B⊐ ⊏C⊐ ⊏D⊐	126	⊏A⊐ ⊏B⊐ ⊏C⊐ ⊏D⊐
27	⊏A⊐ ⊏B⊐ ⊏C⊐ ⊏D⊐	77	⊏A⊐ ⊏B⊐ ⊏C⊐ ⊏D⊐	127	⊏A⊐ ⊏B⊐ ⊏C⊐ ⊏D⊐
28	⊏A⊐ ⊏B⊐ ⊏C⊐ ⊏D⊐	78	⊏A⊐ ⊏B⊐ ⊏C⊐ ⊏D⊐	128	⊏A⊐ ⊏B⊐ ⊏C⊐ ⊏D⊐
29	⊏A⊐ ⊏B⊐ ⊏C⊐ ⊏D⊐	79	⊏A⊐ ⊏B⊐ ⊏C⊐ ⊏D⊐	129	⊏A⊐ ⊏B⊐ ⊏C⊐ ⊏D⊐
30	⊏A⊐ ⊏B⊐ ⊏C⊐ ⊏D⊐	80	⊏A⊐ ⊏B⊐ ⊏C⊐ ⊏D⊐	130	⊏A⊐ ⊏B⊐ ⊏C⊐ ⊏D⊐
31	⊏A⊐ ⊏B⊐ ⊏C⊐ ⊏D⊐	81	⊏A⊐ ⊏B⊐ ⊏C⊐ ⊏D⊐	131	⊏A⊐ ⊏B⊐ ⊏C⊐ ⊏D⊐
32	⊏A⊐ ⊏B⊐ ⊏C⊐ ⊏D⊐	82	⊏A⊐ ⊏B⊐ ⊏C⊐ ⊏D⊐	132	⊏A⊐ ⊏B⊐ ⊏C⊐ ⊏D⊐
33	⊏A⊐ ⊏B⊐ ⊏C⊐ ⊏D⊐	83	⊏A⊐ ⊏B⊐ ⊏C⊐ ⊏D⊐	133	⊏A⊐ ⊏B⊐ ⊏C⊐ ⊏D⊐
34	⊏A⊐ ⊏B⊐ ⊏C⊐ ⊏D⊐	84	⊏A⊐ ⊏B⊐ ⊏C⊐ ⊏D⊐	134	⊏A⊐ ⊏B⊐ ⊏C⊐ ⊏D⊐
35	⊏A⊐ ⊏B⊐ ⊏C⊐ ⊏D⊐	85	⊏A⊐ ⊏B⊐ ⊏C⊐ ⊏D⊐	135	⊏A⊐ ⊏B⊐ ⊏C⊐ ⊏D⊐
36	⊏A⊐ ⊏B⊐ ⊏C⊐ ⊏D⊐	86	⊏A⊐ ⊏B⊐ ⊏C⊐ ⊏D⊐	136	⊏A⊐ ⊏B⊐ ⊏C⊐ ⊏D⊐
37	⊏A⊐ ⊏B⊐ ⊏C⊐ ⊏D⊐	87	⊏A⊐ ⊏B⊐ ⊏C⊐ ⊏D⊐	137	⊏A⊐ ⊏B⊐ ⊏C⊐ ⊏D⊐
38	⊏A⊐ ⊏B⊐ ⊏C⊐ ⊏D⊐	88	⊏A⊐ ⊏B⊐ ⊏C⊐ ⊏D⊐	138	⊏A⊐ ⊏B⊐ ⊏C⊐ ⊏D⊐
39	⊏A⊐ ⊏B⊐ ⊏C⊐ ⊏D⊐	89	⊏A⊐ ⊏B⊐ ⊏C⊐ ⊏D⊐	139	⊏A⊐ ⊏B⊐ ⊏C⊐ ⊏D⊐
40	⊏A⊐ ⊏B⊐ ⊏C⊐ ⊏D⊐	90	⊏A⊐ ⊏B⊐ ⊏C⊐ ⊏D⊐	140	⊏A⊐ ⊏B⊐ ⊏C⊐ ⊏D⊐
41	⊏A⊐ ⊏B⊐ ⊏C⊐ ⊏D⊐	91	⊏A⊐ ⊏B⊐ ⊏C⊐ ⊏D⊐	141	⊏A⊐ ⊏B⊐ ⊏C⊐ ⊏D⊐
42	⊏A⊐ ⊏B⊐ ⊏C⊐ ⊏D⊐	92	⊏A⊐ ⊏B⊐ ⊏C⊐ ⊏D⊐	142	⊏A⊐ ⊏B⊐ ⊏C⊐ ⊏D⊐
43	⊏A⊐ ⊏B⊐ ⊏C⊐ ⊏D⊐	93	⊏A⊐ ⊏B⊐ ⊏C⊐ ⊏D⊐	143	⊏A⊐ ⊏B⊐ ⊏C⊐ ⊏D⊐
44	⊏A⊐ ⊏B⊐ ⊏C⊐ ⊏D⊐	94	⊏A⊐ ⊏B⊐ ⊏C⊐ ⊏D⊐	144	⊏A⊐ ⊏B⊐ ⊏C⊐ ⊏D⊐
45	⊏A⊐ ⊏B⊐ ⊏C⊐ ⊏D⊐	95	⊏A⊐ ⊏B⊐ ⊏C⊐ ⊏D⊐	145	⊏A⊐ ⊏B⊐ ⊏C⊐ ⊏D⊐
46	⊏A⊐ ⊏B⊐ ⊏C⊐ ⊏D⊐	96	⊏A⊐ ⊏B⊐ ⊏C⊐ ⊏D⊐	146	⊏A⊐ ⊏B⊐ ⊏C⊐ ⊏D⊐
47	⊏A⊐ ⊏B⊐ ⊏C⊐ ⊏D⊐	97	⊏A⊐ ⊏B⊐ ⊏C⊐ ⊏D⊐	147	⊏A⊐ ⊏B⊐ ⊏C⊐ ⊏D⊐
48	⊏A⊐ ⊏B⊐ ⊏C⊐ ⊏D⊐	98	⊏A⊐ ⊏B⊐ ⊏C⊐ ⊏D⊐	148	⊏A⊐ ⊏B⊐ ⊏C⊐ ⊏D⊐
49	⊏A⊐ ⊏B⊐ ⊏C⊐ ⊏D⊐	99	⊏A⊐ ⊏B⊐ ⊏C⊐ ⊏D⊐	149	⊏A⊐ ⊏B⊐ ⊏C⊐ ⊏D⊐
50	⊏A⊐ ⊏B⊐ ⊏C⊐ ⊏D⊐	100	⊏A⊐ ⊏B⊐ ⊏C⊐ ⊏D⊐	150	⊏A⊐ ⊏B⊐ ⊏C⊐ ⊏D⊐

Blackstone's Police Sergeants' and Inspectors' Mock Examination Paper 2023

Pack 2

Contents

i. Marking Instructions and Marking Matrix

ii. Answer Booklet

DO NOT OPEN THIS ANSWER PACK UNTIL YOU HAVE COMPLETED THE MOCK EXAM

Marking Instructions

Lay your answer sheet next to the following marking matrix; you may find it useful to fold the answer sheet to do this. Starting with Question 1, compare your marked answer (in the following example this is 'A') with the correct answer given on the marking matrix. If the correct answer matches your marked answer, put a '1' inside the white box on the relevant row. If it does not (see Question 2 following), put a '0'.

Please follow these instructions carefully to ensure accuracy. Marks ('1' or '0') should only be made in the white blank boxes (which indicate the subject area a question is related to)—please do not write anything in the grey boxes.

Question No.	Correct Answer	Crime	Evidence and Procedure	General Police Duties	Excluded Question
1	A			1	
2	B			0	
3	B	1			
4	B				
5	C		0		
6	A				
7	C				0

1 ◼A◼ ⊏B⊐ ⊏C⊐ ⊏D⊐
2 ⊏A⊐ ⊏B⊐ ◼C◼ ⊏D⊐
3 ⊏A⊐ ◼B◼ ⊏C⊐ ⊏D⊐
4 ⊏A⊐ ◼B◼ ⊏C⊐ ⊏D⊐
5 ◼A◼ ⊏B⊐ ⊏C⊐ ⊏D⊐
6 ⊏A⊐ ⊏B⊐ ⊏C⊐ ◼D◼
7 ⊏A⊐ ◼B◼ ⊏C⊐ ⊏D⊐

When you have marked the first 50 questions, add up the total for each column (Crime, Evidence and Procedure and Road Policing) and enter the totals into the boxes marked A1, B1 etc. Then transfer these totals into the corresponding box ('A1', 'B1' etc.) on the score sheet.

48	B				
49	A				
50	C				
Totals		A1 4	B1 2	C1 3	E1 1

Crime	A1	4	A2		A3		**Total** (out of 51) (= A1 + A2 + A3)	
Evidence and Procedure	B1	2	B2		B3		**Total** (out of 37) (= B1 + B2 + B3)	
General Police Duties	C1	3	C2		C3		**Total** (out of 52) (= C1 + C2 + C3)	
							Total questions right (out of 140)	

Then do the same for Questions 51 to 100 and fill in boxes A2 to C2 on the score sheet, and finally Questions 101 to 150, which will enable you to fill in boxes A3 to C3 on the score sheet.

Total up A1 + A2 + A3, which will give you a score for Crime. Then do the same for Evidence and Procedure, and General Police Duties. You will then have a total for each subject area, which you can add up to reach a final total for the whole exam.

Compare your final total to the table underneath the score sheet, which will indicate whether or not you have passed the mock examination.

The target mark for the sergeants' examination is 77 (55%).

The target mark for the inspectors' examination is 91 (65%).

Question No.	Correct Answer	Crime	Evidence and Procedure	General Police Duties	Excluded Question
1	D				
2	C				
3	C				
4	B				
5	B				
6	A				
7	C				
8	B				
9	D				
10	C				
11	B				
12	B				
13	A				
14	C				
15	A				
16	A				
17	A				
18	A				
19	C				
20	C				
21	B				
22	C				
23	C				
24	B				
25	B				
26	D				
27	D				
28	C				
29	C				
30	C				
31	A				
32	B				
33	D				
34	C				
35	B				
36	B				
37	A				
38	A				
39	A				
40	C				
41	B				
42	B				
43	C				
44	D				
45	D				
46	A				
47	B				
48	B				
49	A				
50	C				
Totals		A1	B1	C1	E1

Question No.	Correct Answer	Crime	Evidence and Procedure	General Police Duties	Excluded Question
51	B				
52	C				
53	A				
54	B				
55	B				
56	A				
57	B				
58	B				
59	D				
60	D				
61	B				
62	C				
63	B				
64	A				
65	B				
66	D				
67	C				
68	A				
69	D				
70	A				
71	A				
72	C				
73	A				
74	B				
75	A				
76	D				
77	A				
78	A				
79	B				
80	D				
81	D				
82	A				
83	B				
84	B				
85	C				
86	B				
87	C				
88	A				
89	D				
90	C				
91	C				
92	B				
93	A				
94	C				
95	D				
96	D				
97	B				
98	C				
99	C				
100	A				
Totals		A2	B2	C2	E2

Question No.	Correct Answer	Crime	Evidence and Procedure	General Police Duties	Excluded Question
101	D				
102	C				
103	A				
104	A				
105	C				
106	C				
107	D				
108	A				
109	B				
110	D				
111	D				
112	A				
113	D				
114	A				
115	B				
116	C				
117	B				
118	D				
119	C				
120	C				
121	D				
122	A				
123	B				
124	D				
125	B				
126	B				
127	D				
128	A				
129	C				
130	C				
131	C				
132	A				
133	C				
134	A				
135	D				
136	A				
137	A				
138	D				
139	B				
140	D				
141	D				
142	B				
143	C				
144	B				
145	C				
146	A				
147	C				
148	C				
149	B				
150	D				
Totals		A3	B3	C3	E3

Score Sheet

(Please note that your score for excluded questions is not included on this score sheet.)

Crime	A1		A2		A3		**Total** (out of 51) (= A1 + A2 + A3)	
Evidence and Procedure	B1		B2		B3		**Total** (out of 37) (= B1 + B2 + B3)	
General Police Duties	C1		C2		C3		**Total** (out of 52) (= C1 + C2 + C3)	
							Total questions right (out of 140)	

Questions right	% score	Questions right	% score	Questions right	% score	Questions right	% score	Questions right	% score
1	0.714	29	20.714	57	40.714	85	60.714	113	80.714
2	1.428	30	21.428	58	41.428	86	61.428	114	81.428
3	2.142	31	22.142	59	42.142	87	62.142	115	82.142
4	2.857	32	22.857	60	42.857	88	62.857	116	82.857
5	3.571	33	23.571	61	43.571	89	63.571	117	83.571
6	4.285	34	24.285	62	44.285	90	64.285	118	84.285
7	5	35	25	63	45	91	65 (pass)	119	85
8	5.714	36	25.714	64	45.714	92	65.714	120	85.714
9	6.428	37	26.428	65	46.428	93	66.428	121	86.428
10	7.142	38	27.142	66	47.142	94	67.142	122	87.142
11	7.857	39	27.857	67	47.857	95	67.857	123	87.857
12	8.571	40	28.571	68	48.571	96	68.571	124	88.571
13	9.285	41	29.285	69	49.285	97	69.285	125	89.285
14	10	42	30	70	50	98	70	126	90
15	10.714	43	30.714	71	50.714	99	70.714	127	90.714
16	11.428	44	31.428	72	51.428	100	71.428	128	91.428
17	12.142	45	32.142	73	52.142	101	72.142	129	92.142
18	12.857	46	32.857	74	52.857	102	72.857	130	92.857
19	13.571	47	33.571	75	53.571	103	73.571	131	93.571
20	14.285	48	34.285	76	54.285	104	74.285	132	94.285
21	15	49	35	77	55 (pass)	105	75	133	95
22	15.714	50	35.714	78	55.714	106	75.714	134	95.714
23	16.428	51	36.428	79	56.428	107	76.428	135	96.428
24	17.142	52	37.142	80	57.142	108	77.142	136	97.142
25	17.857	53	37.857	81	57.857	109	77.857	137	97.857
26	18.571	54	38.571	82	58.571	110	78.571	138	98.571
27	19.285	55	39.285	83	59.285	111	79.285	139	99.285
28	20	56	40	84	60	112	80	140	100

Answer Booklet

1. Answer **D** — Answer B is incorrect as s. 14ZA of the Public Order Act 1986 provides powers to deal with 'one-person' protests. Section 14ZA states:

   (1) Subsection (2) applies if the senior police officer, having regard to the time or place at which and the circumstances in which any one-person protest in England and Wales is being carried on or is intended to be carried on, reasonably believes—
      (a) that the noise generated by the person carrying on the protest may result in serious disruption to the activities of an organisation which are carried on in the vicinity of the protest, or
      (b) that—
         (i) the noise generated by the person carrying on the protest may have a relevant impact on persons in the vicinity of the protest, and
         (ii) that impact may be significant.

   The provisions of s. 14ZA(1) do not require any reasonable belief in relation to serious public order or damage to property in order to impose them (answer C is incorrect). Answer A is incorrect as the 'senior police officer' means, in relation to a one-person protest being held or to a one-person protest intended to be held in a case where a person is in a place with a view to carrying on such a protest, the most senior in rank of the police officers present at the scene, or in any other case the chief officer of police (s. 14ZA(5)). Answer D is correct as s. 14ZA(2) states that the senior police officer may give directions imposing on the person organising or carrying on the protest such conditions as appear to the officer necessary to prevent such disruption or impact.

   General Police Duties, para. 3.8.4.5

2. Answer **C** — The Magistrates' Courts Rules 1981, r. 99, as amended by the Magistrates' Courts (Amendment) Rules 2019 (SI 2019/1367), states:

   (1) Subject to paragraph (7), a summons requiring a person to appear before a magistrates' court may be served by—
      (a) handing it to the person in person or, where the person is a corporation, to a person holding a senior position in that corporation;
      (b) posting it to the person at an address where it is reasonably believed that the person

will receive it or, where the person is a corporation, the address for service in accordance with paragraph (2);

(c) addressing it to the person and leaving it for the person at an address where it is reasonably believed that the person will receive it;

(d) where the person has given an electronic address and has not refused to accept service at that address, sending it by electronic means to the address which the person has given;

(e) where the person to be served is given access to an electronic address at which a document may be deposited and has not refused to accept service by the deposit of a document at that address, by depositing it at that address and making it possible for the recipient to read the document, or view or listen to its content, as the case may be, and notifying the recipient of the deposit of the document (which notice may be given by electronic means);

(f) where the person is in custody, sending it to his or her custodian, addressed to the person;

(g) where the person has given a document exchange (DX) box number, and has not refused to accept service by DX, addressing it to the person at that DX box number and leaving it at that document exchange;

(h) where the person is legally represented, serving it on the person's legal representative in the same manner as it could be served on the person under subparagraphs (a), (b), (c) and (g);

(i) where the person is legally represented and the person's legal representative has given an electronic address, sending it to that address;

(j) where the person to be served is legally represented and the legal representative is given access to an electronic address at which a document may be deposited by depositing it at that address and making it possible for the recipient to read the document, or view or listen to its content, as the case may be, and notifying the recipient of the deposit of the document (which notice may be given by electronic means); or

(k) any other method specified by the court.

Answer A is incorrect as the documents can be served on RANKINE's legal representative. Answer B is incorrect as the documents can be served on RANKINE. Answer D is incorrect as the documents can be served electronically. The documents can be served on RANKINE or FINLEY (correct answer C).

Evidence and Procedure, para. 2.1.3

3. Answer **C** — Robbery is committed when a person steals and immediately before or at the time of doing so, and in order to do so, they use force on any person or put or seek to put any person in fear of being then and there subjected to force. What this means is that when force is threatened the person being threatened must fear force for *him/herself and not for another*. So when the gun is pointed towards the back of the customer, the cashier cannot fear force on the customer's behalf meaning that at points A and B no offence of robbery has been committed.

When force is used, it can be used on *anyone* in order to commit the theft. So when CLARKE hits the customer, force is being used on *any person* in order to commit a theft. When the cashier hands over the money, at that point the offence of robbery is complete, making answer D incorrect.

Crime, para. 1.14.3

4. Answer **B** — Where a person is arrested at any place other than a police station, or taken into custody by a constable following an arrest made by a civilian, the constable is normally obliged to take that person to a designated police station (Police and Criminal Evidence Act 1984, s. 30(1), (1A), (1B) and (2)), or in certain circumstances to a non-designated police station ((s. 30(3) to (6)). An arrested person may, instead of being taken to a police station, be released with bail (known as 'street bail') or without bail to attend at a police station at a later date—this makes answer A incorrect. Answer C is incorrect as the fact that the offence of theft is an indictable offence does not impact on PC HUTTON's ability to grant 'street bail'. Section 30A(3B) enables the officer granting bail to consider attaching conditions relevant and proportionate to the suspect and the offence. The conditions that may be considered are the same as those available to a custody officer as contained in s. 3A(5) of the 1976 Act, except for those specified in s. 30A(3A)—this makes answer D incorrect. A police officer of the rank of inspector or above must authorise the release on bail having considered any representations made by the person (s. 30(1A)) and the correct answer at option B.

Evidence and Procedure, paras 2.2.2 to 2.2.2.1

5. Answer **B** — Section 21A of the Criminal Procedure and Investigations Act 1996 introduced a Code of Practice for Arranging and Conducting Interviews of Witnesses Notified by the Accused. The Code sets out guidance that police officers and other persons charged with investigating offences must follow if they arrange or conduct interviews of proposed witnesses whose details are disclosed to the prosecution under the 1996 Act. If an investigator wishes to interview a witness, the witness must be asked whether they consent to being interviewed and informed that an interview is being requested following their identification by the accused as a proposed witness under s. 6A(2) or s. 6C of the Act and that they are not obliged to attend the proposed interview (correct answer B). The witness should be informed that they are entitled to be accompanied by a solicitor at the interview (making answer A incorrect) but nothing in this Code of Practice creates any duty on the part of the Legal Services Commission to provide funding for any such attendance (making answer C incorrect). Answer D is incorrect as there is no requirement for the interviewing officer to be of any specific rank.

Evidence and Procedure, para. 2.5.11.7

6. Answer **A** — Where a person is threatened with death or serious physical injury unless he/she carries out a criminal act, he/she may have a defence of duress (*R v Graham* [1982] 1 WLR 294). If defendants knowingly expose themselves to a risk of such a threat of death or serious physical injury, they cannot claim duress as a defence. So if a person joins a violent gang or an active terrorist organisation, he/she cannot claim duress as a defence to any crimes he/she may go on to commit under threat of death or serious injury from another member or rival of that organisation (*R v Sharp* [1987] QB 853). However, if the purpose of the organisation or gang is not predominantly violent or dangerous (e.g. a gang of shoplifters—or in this case burglars), the defence of duress *may* be available in relation to offences committed while under threat of death or serious physical injury from other gang members (*R v Shepherd* (1987) 86 Cr App R 47)—this eliminates option D. However, as the defence is not available in respect of an offence of murder (*R v Howe* [1987] AC 417) or attempted murder (*R v Gotts* [1992] 2 AC 412) as a principal or secondary offender, that eliminates options B and C leaving A as the correct answer.

Crime, para. 1.4.3

7. Answer **C** — Section 25(1) of the Theft Act 1968 states that a person shall be guilty of an offence of going equipped if, when not at their place of abode, they have with them any article for use in the course of or in connection with any burglary or theft. Offences of fraud are not included within this definition (possession or control of such articles is subject to a separate offence under s. 6 of the Fraud Act 2006), meaning answer D is incorrect. The offence is directed against acts preparatory to the offences of burglary (contrary to s. 9 of the Theft Act 1968), theft (contrary to s. 1 of the Theft Act 1968) and taking a conveyance (contrary to s. 12 of the Theft Act 1968). 'Theft' includes theft with force which would amount to robbery, meaning that answer A is incorrect. The offence is committed when the person is 'not at their place of abode'—in other words, when they are away from their home. SHERRATT does not live at the bar and the fact that this is not a public place does not change the fact that he has committed the offence. In relation to 'have with him', it would suffice if defendants had the article within their immediate control in their car or bag, at their workplace or on their person, making answer B incorrect. As robbery is covered by the offence, the correct answer is C.

EXCLUDED QUESTION, *Crime*, para. 1.14.10

8. Answer **B** — The Police (Conduct) Regulations 2020 define misconduct and the available misconduct sanctions including the Reflective Practice Review, for addressing low-level misconduct as a performance issue. Misconduct is defined as a breach of the Standards of Professional Behaviour that is so serious as to justify disciplinary action. The lowest misconduct sanction now available is a written warning—so that misconduct is a breach of the Standards so serious as to justify a written warning. If the level of misconduct is lower than this, it must be addressed in the Reflective Practice Review process. This makes answer A incorrect (and answer B correct). At a management meeting, the sanctions available are a written warning or a final written warning (answers C and D are incorrect).

General Police Duties, paras 3.17.1, 3.17.6.10

9. Answer **D** — Section 63(2A) of the Police and Criminal Evidence Act 1984 states that a non-intimate sample may be taken without appropriate consent from a person who is in police detention as a consequence of being arrested for a recordable offence and who has not had a non-intimate sample of the same type and from the same part of the body taken in the course of an investigation of the offence by the police (Code D, para. 6.6(a)), making answer C incorrect. This applies whether the person is a juvenile or not making answer A incorrect. Code D, para. 6.7 states that reasonable force may be used, if necessary, to take a non-intimate sample from a person without their consent and does not require the authority of an inspector or above, making answer B incorrect. Code D, para. 6.10 states that a record will be made of the process and, if force is used, the record will include the circumstances and those present.

Evidence and Procedure, para. 2.7.7.4

10. Answer **C** — The Confiscation of Alcohol (Young Persons) Act 1997, s. 1 states:

(1) Where a constable reasonably suspects that a person in a relevant place is in possession of alcohol, and that either—
    (a) he is under the age of 18; or
    (b) he intends that any of the alcohol should be consumed by a person under the age of 18 in that or any other relevant place; or

(c) a person under the age of 18 who is, or has recently been, with him has recently consumed alcohol in that or any other relevant place, the constable may require him to surrender anything in his possession which is, or which the constable reasonably believes to be, alcohol or a container for such alcohol.

(1AA) A constable who imposes a requirement on a person under subsection (1) shall also require the person to state the person's name and address.

Under s. 1(6), a 'relevant place' is:

- any public place, other than licensed premises; or
- any place, other than a public place, to which that person has unlawfully gained access.

There is no requirement for the officer to be in uniform (meaning answer B is incorrect). No authorisation is required for a police officer to utilise this power, meaning that answer D is incorrect. The officer can require the surrender of the alcohol from BOWDEN and OSMAN and require them to state their names and addresses, making answer A incorrect and answer C correct.

General Police Duties, para. 3.6.11.3

11. Answer **B** — The custody officer should record any comment the detainee makes in relation to the arresting officer's account, but shall not invite comment (Code C, para. 3.4); this makes answer C incorrect (and answer B correct, of course). The custody officer shall not put specific questions to the detainee regarding their involvement in any offence nor in respect of any comments made in response to the arresting officer's account, making answers A and D incorrect.

Evidence and Procedure, para. 2.6.7

12. Answer **B** — Section 16 of the Offences Against the Person Act 1861 states that a person who, without lawful excuse, makes to another a threat, intending that the other will fear that it will be carried out, to kill that other or a third person shall be guilty of an offence. The fact that WEIGHTMAN does not believe the threat is immaterial (making answer A incorrect). It can be committed via delivery of the threat to a third party (making answer C incorrect). It does not matter that the threat is made to kill at some time in the future—it is the intention to create the fear in the mind of another that is all important (making answer D incorrect).

Crime, para. 1.10.9

13. Answer **A** — The defence of duress is not available in respect of an offence of murder (*R* v *Howe* [1987] AC 417). Answer C is incorrect as the threat can be made to 'loved ones'. Answer B is incorrect as although the threat drove ALI to commit the offence, that is just one of the requirements and answer A supersedes this. Answer D is not correct as the requirement relating to time (imminently) relates to the threatened injury to the defendant or his/her 'loved ones'.

Crime, para. 1.4.5

14. Answer **C** — To commit a s. 9(1)(a) burglary, the offender must enter a building or part of a building as a trespasser with the intention of stealing anything therein, committing grievous bodily harm or criminal damage—DOOLEY had none of these intentions so a s. 9(1)(a) offence is not committed, making answer A incorrect. Answer B is incorrect as an aggravated burglary

is an aggravated version of the s. 9(1)(a) offence or the s. 9(1)(b) offence. We have established that DOOLEY has not committed a s. 9(1)(a) offence and that remains the case when he enters the lounge. As a s. 9(1)(a) can only be committed at the point of entry, no aggravated s. 9(1)(a) has been committed. Inside the lounge, he can only commit a s. 9(1)(b) burglary—having entered a building or part of a building as a trespasser, he steals or attempts to steal, commits or attempts to commit grievous bodily harm. He has not done anything that fits the s. 9(1)(b) offence so when he picks up the poker, this is not a burglary. However, when he picks up the poker he decides to use it to cause grievous bodily harm and at that stage the poker becomes a weapon of offence (instant arming). When he moves from the lounge into the hallway, he enters part of a building (the hallway) as a trespasser and at that stage he intends to cause LOW grievous bodily harm—this is a s. 9(1)(a) burglary. At the time of the s. 9(1)(a), he has with him a weapon of offence and consequently commits an aggravated burglary at that stage (answer C) making answer D incorrect.

Crime, paras 1.14.5 to 1.14.5.6

15. Answer **A** — Section 28 of the Violent Crime Reduction Act 2006 states:

    (1) A person is guilty of an offence if—
       (a) he uses another to look after, hide or transport a dangerous weapon for him; and
       (b) he does so under arrangements or in circumstances that facilitate, or are intended to facilitate, the weapon's being available to him for an unlawful purpose.
    (2) For the purposes of this section the cases in which a dangerous weapon is to be regarded as available to a person for an unlawful purpose include any case where—
       (a) the weapon is available for him to take possession of it at a time and place; and
       (b) his possession of the weapon at that time and place would constitute, or be likely to involve or to lead to, the commission by him of an offence.

    It appears, on the face of it, that GLINSKI has committed the offence. However, a 'dangerous weapon' means a firearm other than an air weapon or a component part of, or accessory to, an air weapon; or a weapon to which s. 141 or 141A of the Criminal Justice Act 1988 applies. So whilst the offence does relate to firearms (making answer B incorrect), it does not relate to air weapons (making answers C and D incorrect).

    Crime, para. 1.7.11.6

16. Answer **A** — If an authorising officer, of superintendent rank or above, considers that access to a solicitor will interfere with evidence relating to an indictable offence, then access to that solicitor may be delayed, making answer D incorrect. This authorisation to delay access is not a 'blanket' authorisation to deny access to all legal advisers and in the example given in the question, the authorising officer should consider offering the detained person access to another solicitor on the Duty Solicitor scheme, making answer C incorrect. The consultation with a solicitor must be in private (Code C, para. 6.1). In *Brennan* v *United Kingdom* (2001) 34 EHRR 507, the court held that a suspect's right to communicate confidentially with a solicitor 'is part of the basic requirements of a fair trial'. The court found that there had been a breach of Article 6(3)(c) because a police officer had been present during a suspect's first interview with his solicitor, making answer B incorrect.

    Evidence and Procedure, paras 2.6.10, 2.6.20

17. Answer **A** — The Road Traffic Act 1988, s. 163 states:

(1) A person driving a mechanically propelled vehicle on a road must stop the vehicle on being required to do so by a constable in uniform or a traffic officer.

(2) A person riding a cycle on a road must stop the cycle on being required to do so by a constable in uniform or a traffic officer.

(3) If a person fails to comply with this section he is guilty of an offence.

The power is therefore available to the officer (s. 163(2)) making answers B, C and D incorrect.

General Police Duties, para. 3.20.2

18. Answer **A** — The Youth Justice and Criminal Evidence Act 1999 provides that both prosecution and defence witnesses are eligible for special measures, and the categories of eligibility include:

- all witnesses under the age of 18 at the time of the hearing or video recording (s. 16(1)(a));
- vulnerable witnesses who are affected by a mental disorder, impairment of intelligence and social functioning (s. 16(2)(a)(i), (ii));
- vulnerable witnesses who are affected by physical disability or disorder (s. 16(2)(b));
- witnesses in fear or distress about testifying (s. 17(1));
- any witness to a 'relevant offence', currently defined to include homicide offences and other offences involving a firearm or knife (s. 17(5)–(7), sch. 1A);
- adult victims of domestic violence who are vulnerable or intimidated;
- adult complainants of sexual offences (as defined by s. 62 of the 1999 Act), human trafficking offences (s. 59A of the Sexual Offences Act 2003 or s. 4 of the Asylum and Immigration (Treatment of Claimants, etc.) Act 2004), indecent photographs of children offences (s. 1 of the Protection of Children Act 1978 (take, permit to be taken or publish etc. such a photograph), s. 160 of the Criminal Justice Act 1988 (possession of such a photograph)), slavery and trafficking offences (ss. 1 and 2 of the Modern Slavery Act 2015) and an offence of domestic abuse under the Domestic Abuse Act 2021.

The eligibility criteria means that answer D is incorrect. In relation to the category 'any witness to a "relevant offence" involving a firearm, offensive weapon or knife', the 'relevant offence' is an offence specified in sch. 1A to the 1999 Act that includes murder, manslaughter, wounding, assault etc. All witnesses involved in such cases, including police officers, are automatically eligible for a special measures direction unless they decline (s. 17(5)), this means that answer B is incorrect. Answer C is incorrect as the primary rule is that all witnesses under the age of 18, regardless of the nature of the offence charged, are eligible for their evidence to be given by video interview and the use of live link; this does not prohibit a child witness who wishes to testify in court (ss. 21 and 22) (correct answer A).

Evidence and Procedure, para. 2.3.9.1

19. Answer **C** — Powers to enter under s. 17 are available to officers for many reasons. Pursuing a person who is unlawfully at large and whom the officer is pursuing is one of those reasons (s. 17(1)(d)) as is the power to enter, search and arrest for an indictable offence (s. 17(1)(b))—but these are not the only reasons an officer may enter under s. 17, meaning that answers B and D are incorrect. The Police and Criminal Evidence Act 1984, s. 17(1)(c)(iii) states that a constable

may enter and search any premises for the purpose of arresting a person for an offence under s. 4 of the Public Order Act 1986 (fear or provocation of violence). The officer does not have to be in uniform to exercise the power under s. 17(1)(c)(iii), making answer A incorrect. Force may be used if necessary, meaning that answer C is correct.

General Police Duties, para. 3.2.5.1

20. Answer **C** — The Child Abduction Act 1984, s. 1 states:

    (1) Subject to subsections (5) and (8) below, a person connected with a child under the age of 16 commits an offence if he takes or sends the child out of the United Kingdom without the appropriate consent.

    Answer A is incorrect as the offence applies to a child under the age of 16. Answer B is incorrect as the offence is only committed if the child is taken out of the United Kingdom so taking Jane to Scotland would not amount to an offence.

    The Child Abduction Act 1984, s. 1 states:

    (4) A person does not commit an offence under this section by taking or sending a child out of the United Kingdom without obtaining the appropriate consent if—
        (a) he is a person named in a child arrangements order as a person with whom the child is to live, and he takes or sends the child out of the United Kingdom for a period of less than one month; or
        (b) he is a special guardian of the child and he takes or sends the child out of the United Kingdom for a period of less than three months.

    As Kate AMBLER is a person named in a child arrangements order and she has taken Jane out of the country for less than one month, she does not commit the offence (correct answer C), making D incorrect.

Crime, paras 1.13.2 to 1.13.2.2

21. Answer **B** — The Public Order Act 1986, s. 29B states:

    (1) A person who uses threatening words or behaviour, or displays any written material which is threatening, is guilty of an offence if he intends thereby to stir up religious hatred or hatred on the grounds of sexual orientation.
    (2) An offence under this section is committed in a public or private place, except that no offence is committed where the words or behaviour are used, or the written material is displayed, by a person inside a dwelling and are not heard or seen except by other persons in that or another dwelling.

    In proceedings for an offence under this section, it is a defence for the accused to prove that he/she was inside a dwelling and that he/she had no reason to believe that the words or behaviour used, or the written material displayed, would be heard or seen by a person outside that or any other dwelling.

    These circumstances do not amount to an offence (correct answer B)—s. 29B(2) states that 'no offence is committed' when the written material is displayed by a person inside a dwelling (BERRY) and not seen except by other persons in that or another dwelling (KAPLAN). This means that answers A and C are incorrect—no offence has been committed. Answer D is incorrect as even if BERRY did intend to stir up religious hatred by displaying the flag, s. 29B(2) means that no offence is committed.

General Police Duties, para. 3.12.2.5

22. Answer **C** — Code A of the Codes of Practice (para. 4.5) states that a record is required for each person and each vehicle searched. However, if a person is in a vehicle and both are searched, and the object and grounds of the search are the same, only one record needs to be completed (meaning answer B is incorrect). Answer D is incorrect as no such notice is required (it is if you are searching an unattended vehicle—see Code A, para. 4.8). Answer A is incorrect as if a vehicle is searched and a record of the search has been made, then the owner of the vehicle which was searched or the person who was in charge of the vehicle at the time when it was searched is entitled to a copy of the record of search if they ask for one (s. 3(8))—the entitlement to a copy of the search record will run for three months beginning on the date on which the search was made (s. 3(9)), this means answer C is correct.

General Police Duties, paras 3.1.6.1 to 3.1.6.2

23. Answer **C** — Annex A of Code C deals with intimate searches. Body orifices other than the mouth may be searched under s. 55(1) of PACE only if authorised by an officer of inspector rank or above who has reasonable grounds for believing that the person may have concealed on themselves:

    (a) anything which they could and might use to cause physical injury to themselves or others at the station; or
    (b) a Class A drug which they intended to supply to another or to export;
    (c) and the officer has reasonable grounds for believing that an intimate search is the only means of removing those items.

    A search authorised to locate a Class A drug may only be carried out by a registered medical practitioner or registered nurse (making answers A and D incorrect). Such a search can take place at a hospital, surgery or other medical premises (making answer B incorrect and answer C correct).

Evidence and Procedure, para. 2.6.19

24. Answer **B** — The information of which NEWMAN is in possession would be classed as relating to 'terrorism' as defined in s. 1 of the Terrorism Act 2000. Answer A is incorrect as the disclosure of such information (in England and Wales) must be made to a constable not 'any person in authority'. Answer C is incorrect as s. 38B(6) of the Act means that a person resident in the United Kingdom could be charged with the offence even if he/she was outside the country when he/she became aware of the information. Answer D is incorrect as it is a defence for a person charged with such an offence to prove that he/she had a reasonable excuse for not making the disclosure (s. 38B(4)).

General Police Duties, para. 3.15.4.3

25. Answer **B** — Section 51 of the Criminal Justice and Public Order Act 1994 states:

(1) A person commits an offence if—
   (a) he does an act which intimidates, and is intended to intimidate, another person ('the victim'),
   (b) he does the act knowing or believing that the victim is assisting in the investigation of an offence or is a witness or *potential witness* or a juror or potential juror in proceedings for an offence, and
   (c) he does it intending thereby to cause the investigation or the course of justice to be obstructed, perverted or interfered with.

(2) A person commits an offence if—
   (a) he does an act which harms, and is intended to harm, another person or, intending to cause another person to fear harm, he threatens to do an act which would harm that other person,
   (b) he does or threatens to do the act knowing or believing that the person harmed or threatened to be harmed ('the victim'), or some other person, *has assisted* in an investigation into an offence or *has given evidence or particular evidence* in proceedings for an offence, or *has acted* as a juror or concurred in a particular verdict in proceedings for an offence, and
   (c) he does or threatens to do it because of that knowledge or belief.

(3) For the purposes of subsections (1) and (2) it is immaterial that the act is or would be done, or that the threat is made—
   (a) otherwise than in the presence of the victim, or
   (b) to a person other than the victim.

(4) The harm that may be done or threatened may be financial as well as physical (whether to the person or a person's property) and similarly as respects an intimidatory act which consists of threats.

The offence can be committed against a 'potential witness', making answer A incorrect. The victim of the offence does not actually have to be intimidated, so even if the victim is not in fear, the offence can be made out, making answer C incorrect. In this question, the offence is committed when DORMLEY makes the threat to ESTERTON regarding wages and also when he threatens ESTERTON with violence. Answer D is incorrect as ESTERTON has not actually assisted in an investigation etc.

General Police Duties, para. 3.14.5.1

26. Answer **D** — The offence of misconduct in a public office applies to any person holding a public office and WEIR would be included in that category. In *R v Bowden* [1996] 1 WLR 98, a man employed by a local council as a maintenance manager dishonestly caused his employees to carry out works on his girlfriend's premises and committed the offence, making answers A and B incorrect. To prove the offence, a number of factors must be established including evidence of wilful neglect and/or wilful misconduct. Simple inadvertence or accidental action/ omission without more will not be enough (*Attorney-General's Reference (No. 3 of 2003)* [2004] EWCA Crim 868) meaning that PC JAMES will not have committed the offence and making answer C incorrect.

General Police Duties, para. 3.18.17.1

27. Answer **D** — 'Special defences' are only available to a defendant who is charged with an offence of murder—they cannot be used in answer to any other charge, e.g. attempted murder.

Crime, para. 1.5.3

28. Answer **C** — The 'specified period' of an improvement notice is a period specified by the manager conducting the meeting (having considered any representations made by or on behalf of the police officer) within which the police officer must improve his/her performance or attendance. It is expected that the specified period for improvement would not normally exceed *three months* (correct answer C). This makes answer A incorrect. Answer B is incorrect as on the application of the police officer or otherwise (e.g. on the application of his/her line manager), the appropriate authority may extend the specified period, if it considers it appropriate to do so. In setting an extension to the specified period, consideration should be given to any known periods of extended absence from the police officer's normal role, e.g. if the police officer is going to be on long periods of pre-planned holiday leave, study leave or is due to undergo an operation. The extension should not lead to the improvement period exceeding *12 months* (making answer D incorrect) unless the appropriate authority is satisfied that there are exceptional circumstances making this appropriate.

General Police Duties, para. 3.18.9.2

29. Answer **C** — A person commits an offence under s. 12 if, without having the consent of the owner or other lawful authority, he/she takes any conveyance for his/her own or another's use or, knowing that any conveyance has been taken without such authority, drives it or allows him/herself to be carried on it. The offence can be committed anywhere, making answer A incorrect. The conveyance must 'convey' you or another because you are in it or on it (or you intend for you or another to use it that way in the future). In this case, FEATHERSTONE *pushes* the car 15 feet—it does not convey him, so he does not commit the offence. This makes answers B and D incorrect. Answer D is further incorrect as the 'lawful authority' element of the offence is not restricted in the way option D suggests; those individuals are mentioned in the *Crime Manual* but only as examples of who might have such lawful authority and not as a definitive list.

Crime, para. 1.14.7

30. Answer **C** — The Confiscation of Alcohol (Young Persons) Act 1997, s. 1 states:

(1) Where a constable reasonably suspects that a person in a relevant place is in possession of alcohol, and that either—
   (a) he is under the age of 18; or
   (b) he intends that any of the alcohol should be consumed by a person under the age of 18 in that or any other relevant place; or
   (c) a person under the age of 18 who is, or has recently been, with him has recently consumed alcohol in that or any other relevant place,
   the constable may require him to surrender anything in his possession which is, or which the constable reasonably believes to be, alcohol or a container for alcohol.

So under s. 1(1), PC BUNN can require the surrender of the opened and unopened cans of cider, making answer B incorrect. Under s. 1(2), the officer may dispose of anything surrendered to him/her in answer to the making of the requirement, making answer D incorrect. Under s. 1(1AB), a constable who imposes a requirement on a person under subs. (1) may, if the constable reasonably suspects that the person is under the age of 16, remove the person to the person's place of residence or a place of safety, making answer A incorrect. Although a 'place of safety' is not defined, this may be a relative or friend or, where necessary, *a police station* or social services accommodation (correct answer C).

General Police Duties, para. 3.6.11.3

31. Answer **A** — Answer A is correct as the officer directing that the powers conferred by s. 16 shall be exercisable will be an officer of the rank of superintendent or above. Answer B is incorrect as the powers apply where the officer has 'reasonable cause to believe' not suspect. Answer C is incorrect as there is no requirement for the constable exercising the power to be in uniform. Answer D is incorrect as the power is available in a public place only.

General Police Duties, para. 3.7.10

32. Answer **B** — The power to issue a domestic violence protection notice (a DVPN) is provided by s. 24 of the Crime and Security Act 2010, which states that a member of a police force not below the rank of superintendent ('the authorising officer') may issue a DVPN under this section (s. 24(1)). Before issuing a DVPN, the authorising officer must, in particular, consider several issues which includes any representations made by the person the notice is made in relation to (in this case, John EDMONSON) as to the issuing of the DVPN (correct answer B). Answer A is incorrect as a DVPN can be issued in circumstances where the person for whose protection it is issued does not consent to the issuing of the DVPN. Answer D is incorrect as the purpose of a DVPN is to secure the immediate protection of a victim of domestic violence and abuse (V) from future violence or a threat of violence from a suspected perpetrator (P). A DVPN prohibits P from molesting V and, where they cohabit, may require P to leave those premises. Where a DVPN has been issued, a constable (not the authorising officer) must apply to a magistrates' court for a Domestic Violence Protection Order (DVPO). The application must be heard by the magistrates' court not later than 48 hours (not 24) after the DVPN was served (s. 27) making answer C incorrect.

EXCLUDED QUESTION, *General Police Duties*, para. 3.11.5

33. Answer **D** — The offence under s. 15 cannot be committed by a person under 18.

Crime, para. 1.12.7.7

34. Answer **C** — Code B, para. 3.4 states that applications for all search warrants must be made with the written authority of an officer of at least the rank of *inspector* (although in urgent cases where such an officer is not readily available, the most senior officer on duty may author-ise the application), making answer A incorrect. Answer B is incorrect as s. 16(3) of PACE states that entry and search under such a warrant must be made within *three* months from the date of its issue. If the warrant is an all premises warrant, no premises which are not specified in it may be entered and searched unless a police officer of at least the rank of *inspector* has, in writing, authorised them to be entered (s. 16(3A)) making answer D incorrect.

General Police Duties, para. 3.2.4

35. Answer **B** — The Police and Criminal Evidence Act 1984 makes provision for the so-called citizen's arrest powers. Far narrower than the police powers, these powers of arrest are set out in s. 24A, which states:

(1) A person other than a constable may arrest without a warrant—
  (a) anyone who is in the act of committing an indictable offence;
  (b) anyone whom he has reasonable grounds for suspecting to be committing an indictable offence.
(2) Where an indictable offence has been committed, a person other than a constable may arrest without a warrant—
  (a) anyone who is guilty of the offence;
  (b) anyone whom he has reasonable grounds for suspecting to be guilty of it.
(3) But the power of summary arrest conferred by subsection (1) or (2) is exercisable only if—
  (a) the person making the arrest has reasonable grounds for believing that for any of the reasons mentioned in subsection (4) it is necessary to arrest the person in question; and
  (b) it appears to the person making the arrest that it is not reasonably practicable for a constable to make it instead.
(4) The reasons are to prevent the person in question:
  (a) causing physical injury to himself or any other person;
  (b) suffering physical injury;
  (c) causing loss of or damage to property; or
  (d) making off before a constable can assume responsibility for him.
(5) This section does not apply in relation to an offence under Part 3 or 3A of the Public Order Act 1986.

Unlike the powers of arrest available to police officers (which apply to any and every offence), the citizen's power of arrest only applies where the relevant offence is indictable. This power is available to police staff and others such as Police Community Support Officers (making answer A incorrect). An offence that is triable either way is an 'indictable offence'—this would only exclude offences that are triable summarily only, making answer C incorrect. LORIMER behaved correctly (answer B) as the grounds under s. 24A(1)(b) applied and were accompanied by the element at s. 24A(3) and (4)(b), making answer D incorrect.

General Police Duties, para. 3.3.8

36. Answer **B** — Section 1(5) of the Public Order Act 1986 states that the offence of riot can be committed in public or private, making answer A incorrect. The offence under s. 1(1) states that where 12 or more persons who are present together use or threaten unlawful violence for a common purpose and the conduct of them (taken together) is such as would cause a person of reasonable firmness present at the scene to fear for their personal safety, each of the persons *using unlawful violence* for the common purpose is guilty of riot. An important point to note is that it is only the persons *using* violence who can be guilty of the offence of riot. You do require 12 or more persons present together for riot but they do not all need to use violence, making answer C incorrect. As it is those who use violence who commit the offence, this makes answer D incorrect and answer B correct.

General Police Duties, para. 3.9.3

37. Answer **A** — Only one criminal damage offence is capable of being racially and/or religiously aggravated ('simple' criminal damage—Criminal Damage Act 1971, s. 1(1)) meaning that answer C is incorrect. Section 28 of the Crime and Disorder Act 1998 states:

(1) An offence is racially or religiously aggravated for the purposes of sections 29 to 32 . . . if—
   (a) at the time of committing the offence, or immediately before or after doing so, the offender demonstrates towards the victim of the offence hostility based on the victim's membership (or presumed membership) of a racial or religious group; or
   (b) the offence is *motivated (wholly or partly) by hostility* towards members of a racial or religious group based on their membership of that group.

As the offence was motivated by religious hostility, answer D is incorrect. A 'presumption' of racial/religious identity may well be wrong—that does not matter, so the fact that NORRIS is not from the religious group LEWIN presumed him to be does not stop the offence being committed therefore answer B is incorrect.

Crime, paras 1.9.2 to 1.9.3.7

38. Answer **A** — Section 6(5) of the Road Traffic Act 1988 states that if an accident occurs owing to the presence of a motor vehicle on a road or other public place and a constable reasonably believes that the person was driving, attempting to drive or in charge of the vehicle at the time of the accident, they may require a preliminary test to take place. You must show that an accident has taken place, not simply believed that to be the case. Answer B is incorrect as, apart from the fact that the requirement cannot be made, the preliminary test may take place at or near the place where the requirement to cooperate with the test is imposed *or*, if the constable who imposes the requirement thinks it expedient to do so, at a police station specified by him/her. Answer C is incorrect as if an accident has taken place there is no need for the officer making the requirement to believe or even suspect that the person has been drinking. Answer D is incorrect as there is no need for the officer to believe or suspect that any offence has taken place.

General Police Duties, para. 3.22.4.3

39. Answer **A** — The doctrine of transferred *mens rea* is not restricted to offences under the Offences Against the Person Act 1861, making answer B incorrect. The issue of transferred *mens rea* can be important in relation to the liability of accessories. If the principal's intentions (BEST) are to be extended to an accessory (FLACK), it must be shown that those intentions were either contemplated and accepted by that person at the time of the offence, or that they were 'transferred'. So transferred *mens rea* is applicable to accessories and answer D is incorrect. An example is provided in the 2022 *Crime Manual* where a person (X) encourages another (Y) to assault Z. Y decides to attack a different person instead. X will not be liable for that assault because it was not contemplated or agreed by X. If, however, in trying to assault Z, Y happens to injure a third person inadvertently, then 'transferred *mens rea*' may result in X being liable for those injuries even though X had no wish for that person to be so injured. In trying to cause criminal damage to STIRLING's car, BEST damages a car owned by DUTTON—FLACK would be liable for that damage but would not be liable for the assault as that was not contemplated by FLACK so answer A is correct and answer C is incorrect.

Crime, para. 1.1.11

40. Answer **C** — Answer A is incorrect as a breach of the peace can take place in private as well as in public. Answer B is incorrect as a breach of the peace occurs when an act is done, or threatened to be done:

- which harms a person or, in his/her presence, his/her property; or
- which is likely to cause such harm; or
- which puts someone in fear of such harm.

A person arrested for a breach of the peace is not in police detention and the provisions in relation to bail do not apply, making answer D incorrect. After being arrested, a person may be detained and placed before the next available court, or detained until there is no further likelihood of a reoccurrence of the breach of the peace.

General Police Duties, paras 3.9.2 to 3.9.2.4

41. Answer **B** — 'Special warnings' do not apply to interviews with suspects who have not been arrested. This makes answers A, C and D incorrect.

Evidence and Procedure, para. 2.8.2.5

42. Answer **B** — Section 4(1A) of the Criminal Law Act 1967 states that a 'relevant offence' means:

(a) an offence for which the sentence is fixed by law,
(b) an offence for which a person of 18 years or over (not previously convicted) may be sentenced to imprisonment for a term of five years (or might be so sentenced but for the restrictions imposed by section 33 of the Magistrates' Courts Act 1980).

Theft is an offence punishable by a term of seven years' imprisonment on conviction making it a 'relevant offence' and making answer D incorrect. This offence must involve some positive act by the defendant; saying or doing nothing will not suffice, making answer A incorrect. For the offence to exist, the defendant must know or believe the assisted person to be guilty of the offence or some relevant offence. Mere suspicion, however strong, that the 'assisted' person had committed a relevant offence will not be enough which means that answer B is correct and that answer C is incorrect.

General Police Duties, para. 3.14.7

43. Answer **C** — Possession of cannabis or khat can be dealt with under the Penalty Notice for Disorder (PND) Scheme (answer A is incorrect). PNDs cannot be issued for any other drug-related offences other than possession of cannabis or cannabis derivatives (answer D is incorrect). PNDs may be issued to any adult found in possession of cannabis for personal use; they are not appropriate for offenders under the age of 18 (answer B is incorrect and answer C is the correct answer).

Crime, para. 1.6.3.7

44. Answer **D** — The Criminal Justice and Courts Act 2015, s. 33 states:

(1) It is an offence for a person to disclose a private sexual photograph or film if the disclosure is made—
    (a) without the consent of an individual who appears in the photograph or film, and
    (b) with the intention of causing that individual distress.
(2) But it is not an offence under this section for the person to disclose the photograph or film to the individual mentioned in subsection (1)(a) and (b).

Answer A is incorrect as WAYMAN intends to cause BAILEY (and not LIGHTFOOT) distress.

Answer B is incorrect as the image can be one that was photographed or filmed and is a still or moving image (or part of an image) originally captured by photography or by the making of a film recording. The offence is committed with the intention that the individual in the photograph or film will be caused distress (making answer C incorrect and answer D correct).

EXCLUDED QUESTION, *Crime*, para. 1.12.20

45. Answer **D** — A Scottish officer may arrest someone suspected of committing an offence in Scotland who is found in England, Wales or Northern Ireland if it would have been lawful to arrest that person had he/she been found in Scotland—this means that answers A and C are incorrect. In such a case, the officer must take the person to a designated police station in Scotland or to the nearest designated police station in England or Wales (s. 137(7) of the Criminal Justice and Public Order Act 1994). This makes answer B incorrect and answer D correct.

General Police Duties, para. 3.3.9.5

46. Answer **A** — A significant statement is one which appears capable of being used in evidence against the suspect, in particular a direct admission of guilt (Code C, para. 11.4A) and must have been made in the presence and hearing of a police officer (or other police staff member) (Code C, para. 11.4)—it could be made at any location (answer B is incorrect). Answer D is incorrect as a 'significant statement' will be made prior to a caution not after it. The suspect must be given the opportunity to clarify, confirm, deny or add to an earlier statement—the statement should be put to the suspect at the beginning of the interview, after caution and before questioning (answer C is incorrect).

Evidence and Procedure, para. 2.8.3

47. Answer **B** — Answer D is incorrect as s. 25(1) of the Criminal Justice and Public Order Act 1994 states that a person who in any proceedings has been charged with or convicted of an offence to which this section applies in circumstances to which it applies shall be granted bail in those proceedings only if the court or, as the case may be, *the constable* considering the grant of bail is of the opinion that there are *exceptional circumstances which justify it*. Section 25 provides that bail may not be granted where a person is charged with one of the offences below and also has a conviction for one of those offences:

(a) murder;
(b) attempted murder;
(c) manslaughter;
(d) rape under the law of Scotland;
(e) an offence under section 1 of the Sexual Offences Act 1956 (rape);
(f) an offence under section 1 of the Sexual Offences Act 2003 (rape);
(g) an offence under section 2 of that Act (assault by penetration);
(h) an offence under section 4 of that Act (causing a person to engage in sexual activity without consent) where the activity caused involved penetration within subsection (4)(a) to (d) of that section;

(i)   an offence under section 5 of that Act (rape of a child under 13);

(j)   an offence under section 6 of that Act (assault of a child under 13 by penetration);

(k)   an offence under section 8 of that Act (causing or inciting a child under 13 to engage in sexual activity), where an activity involving penetration within subsection (3)(a) to (d) of that section was caused;

(l)   an offence under section 30 of that Act (sexual activity with a person with a mental disorder impeding choice), where the touching involved penetration within subsection (3)(a) to (d) of that section;

(m) an offence under section 31 of that Act (causing or inciting a person, with a mental disorder impeding choice, to engage in sexual activity), where an activity involving penetration within subsection (3)(a) to (d) of that section was caused;

…

(n)   an attempt to commit an offence within any of paragraphs (d) to (m).

As BRUSHETT has a conviction for assault by penetration (mentioned at s. 25(2)(g)) and is charged with an offence of sexual activity with a person with a mental disorder impeding choice that involves penetration (mentioned at s. 25(2)(l)), the provisions of s. 25 will be applicable—this eliminates answers A and C.

Evidence and Procedure, para. 2.2.5

48. Answer **B** — Any representation made must be one as to fact or law, so a broken promise is not in itself a false representation. However, a statement may be false if it misrepresents the current intentions or state of mind of the person making it or anyone else. This MCQ is a good example of such behaviour. CROFTON visits WOODWARD's house and tells WOODWARD that he needs emergency work carried out on his roof. CROFTON states that he is in a position to do the work immediately but only if WOODWARD pays him £150 there and then. WOODWARD gives CROFTON the money and CROFTON then leaves without carrying out the work; the truth of the matter is that CROFTON had never intended to carry out the work. Such a 'promise' by CROFTON would amount to an offence as it involved a false representation, i.e. he never intended to keep the promise (this makes answer A incorrect). Answer D is incorrect as the offence is complete the moment the false representation is made. Answer C is incorrect as the mode of trial for the fraud offence is not related to the value of the goods concerned (in a way that you might associate with low-value shoplifting).

Crime, paras 1.15.2 to 1.15.4

49. Answer **A** — Section 1(4) of the Police and Criminal Evidence Act 1984 states that if a person is in a garden or yard occupied with and used for the purposes of a dwelling or on other land so occupied and used, a constable *may not* search him/her in the exercise of the power conferred by this section *unless* the constable has reasonable grounds for believing:

(a)   that he does not reside in the dwelling; and

(b)   that he is not in the place in question with the express or implied permission of a person who resides in the dwelling.

So the power is available if the officer reasonably believes s. 1(4)((a) or (b) above. This means that answer B is incorrect. Answers C and D are incorrect as the power under s. 1 of PACE is *not available in a dwelling in any circumstances* (regardless of the officer's mindset etc.). If the officers reasonably believe s. 1(4)(a) and (b) that means they can search MARTIN but, as you can never use s. 1 in a dwelling, it means that answer A is correct.

General Police Duties, paras 3.1.4.1 to 3.1.4.2

50. Answer **C** — If DELANEY refuses then an inspector can provide oral authorisation that he be examined, although this will have to be confirmed in writing as soon as practicable (Code D, para. 5.8). DELANEY's consent is not required but if it is given then an inspector's authority is not required, making answer D incorrect. The power can be used to establish the identity of an individual or to identify them as a person involved in the commission of an offence, making answer A incorrect. Force can be used if necessary, making answer B incorrect.

Evidence and Procedure, para. 2.8.6

51. Answer **B** — If a defendant intends to kill or cause serious injury to the mother, that intention cannot support a charge of murder in respect of the baby if it goes on to die after being born alive. It may, however, support a charge of manslaughter (*Attorney-General's Reference (No. 3 of 1994)* [1998] AC 245) so this makes answer D incorrect. As TREVINO could be held liable for the death of the child, answers A and C are incorrect.

Crime, para. 1.5.2

52. Answer **C** — The Criminal Justice and Public Order Act 1994, s. 61 states:

(1) If the senior police officer present at the scene reasonably believes that two or more persons are trespassing on land and are present there with the common purpose of residing there for any period, that reasonable steps have been taken by or on behalf of the occupier to ask them to leave and—
   (a) that any of those persons
      (i) in the case of persons trespassing on land in England and Wales, has caused damage, disruption or distress (see subsection 10);
      (ii) in the case of persons trespassing on the land in Scotland,
   has caused to damage to the land or to property on the land or used threatening, abusive or insulting words or behaviour towards the occupier, a member of his family or an employee or agent of his, or
   (b) in either case those persons have between them six or more vehicles on the land,
   he may direct those persons, or any of them, to leave the land and to remove any vehicles or other property they have with them on the land.

The direction can be given if the circumstances at s. 61(1)(a) or (b) apply, meaning that answer B is incorrect. The direction can be given to two or more persons, making answer D incorrect. It can be given if any of those persons has caused damage, disruption or distress and using threatening, abusive or insulting words or behaviour would amount to such 'distress', so answer A is incorrect.

EXCLUDED QUESTION, *General Police Duties*, para. 3.5.4

53. Answer **A** — Section 125CA(3) of the Magistrates' Courts Act 1980 states that a disclosure order is an order requiring the person to whom it is directed to supply the designated officer for the court with any of the following information about the person to whom the warrant relates:

(a) his name, date of birth or national insurance number;
(b) his address (or any of his addresses).

This makes answer A correct and answers B, C and D incorrect.

Evidence and Procedure, para. 2.1.6.1

54. Answer **B** — Section 2 of the Criminal Damage Act 1971 states:

A person who without lawful excuse makes to another a threat, intending that that other would fear it would be carried out—

(a) to destroy or damage any property belonging to that other or a third person; or
(b) to destroy or damage his own property in a way which he knows is likely to endanger the life of that other or a third person;

shall be guilty of an offence.

This is all about the intention of the offender and has nothing whatsoever to do with the 'victim' of the offence. So the fact that SMITH does not believe MANNIGER is immaterial (making answer C incorrect). 'Conditional' threats are relevant to offences of assault but not to threats to commit criminal damage, making answer A incorrect. Answer D is incorrect as the threat was made to SMITH and not INCE. The offence is committed by a person (MANNIGER) who without lawful excuse makes to another (SMITH) a threat, intending that *that* other (SMITH not INCE) would fear that it will be carried out. So the offence is committed because MANNIGER made the threat to SMITH (regardless of what INCE believes/fears—correct answer B).

Crime, para. 1.16.5

55. Answer **B** — The Fraud Act 2006, s. 6 states:

(1) A person is guilty of an offence if he has in his possession or under his control any article for use in the course of or in connection with any fraud.

An 'article' can be anything whatsoever. For the purposes of ss. 6 and 7 of the Act, an 'article' includes any program or data held in electronic form. Examples of cases where electronic programs or data could be used in fraud are:

- a computer program that generates credit card numbers
- a computer template that can be used for producing blank utility bills
- a computer file that contains lists of other people's credit card details.

So the computer program and the template found on EISEMAN's computer are 'articles' for the purposes of s. 6. The offence under s. 6 can be committed anywhere at all, including the home of the defendant (making answer D incorrect). It is committed when the defendant has articles in his/her possession and also when the defendant has them in his/her control, so the defendant may be some distance away from the articles and still commit the offence. The s. 6

offence applies to 'any fraud' which will therefore include all fraud offences under the 2006 Act. However, answers A and C are incorrect and answer B is the correct answer as the offence is only committed in respect of *future offences* and not offences that have already taken place (*R* v *Sakalauskas* [2014] 1 All ER 1231).

Crime, para. 1.15.9

56. Answer **A** — Section 21 of the Firearms Act 1968 places restrictions on convicted persons in respect of their possession of firearms and/or ammunition.

Any person who has been sentenced to:
- custody for *life*; or
- to preventive detention, imprisonment, corrective training, youth custody or detention in a young offender institution for three years or more, must not, *at any time*, have a firearm or ammunition in his/her possession, i.e. a life-time ban.

So s. 21 applies to CONRAD (making answer B incorrect). It does not matter where the possession activity takes place (making answer D incorrect). The ban on possession applies to firearms and ammunition (making answer C incorrect).

Crime, para. 1.7.14

57. Answer **B** — The Malicious Communications Act 1988, s. 1 states:

(1) Any person who sends to another person—
   (a) a letter, electronic communication or article of any description which conveys—
       (i) a message which is indecent or grossly offensive;
       (ii) a threat; or
       (iii) information which is false and known or believed to be false by the sender; or
   (b) any article or electronic communication which is, in whole or part, of an indecent or grossly offensive nature,
   is guilty of an offence if his purpose, or one of his purposes, in sending it is that it should, so far as falling within paragraph (a) or (b) above, cause distress or anxiety to the recipient or to any other person to whom he intends that it or its contents or nature should be communicated.

Answer A is incorrect as the offence covers electronic communications which include any oral or other communication by means of an electronic communications network. This will extend to communications in electronic form such as emails, text messages, pager messages, social media etc. (s. 1(2A)). The nature of the communication could relate to information which is false and known or believed to be false (s. 1(1)(a)(iii)) making answer C incorrect. 'Sending' will include transmitting (note that this offence is complete as soon as the communication is sent) so the correct answer is B and means that answer D is incorrect.

General Police Duties, para. 3.13.9

58. Answer **B** — Paragraph 9.3 of Code C states that detainees should be visited at least every hour. If no reasonable risk was identified in a risk assessment, there is no need to wake a sleeping detainee (making answers C and D incorrect in relation to SHAFIQ). Those suspected of being intoxicated through drink or drugs or having swallowed drugs or whose level

of consciousness causes concern must, subject to any clinical direction given by an appropriate health-care professional, be visited and roused at least every half hour (making answer A incorrect).

Evidence and Procedure, para. 2.6.13

59. Answer **D** — A witness may be taken to a particular neighbourhood or place to see whether they can identify the person they saw. It is not necessary for the witness to be accompanied by two officers, making answer C incorrect. Where it is practicable, a record should be made of the witness's description of the suspect before asking the witness to make an identification in such a manner, so rather than being a bar to taking part in a 'street' identification, the first description is a desirable element, making answer A incorrect. Care must be taken not to direct the witness's attention to any individual unless, taking into account all the circumstances, this cannot be avoided. However, this does not prevent a witness from being asked to look carefully at the people standing around at the time or to look towards a group or in a particular direction if this is necessary to make sure that the witness does not overlook a possible suspect simply because they are looking in the opposite direction, making answer B incorrect. Answer D is correct as the officer has complied with the Codes of Practice (Code D, para. 3.2).

Evidence and Procedure, para. 2.7.4.2

60. Answer **D** — The Sexual Offences Act 2003, s. 1 states:

(1) A person (A) commits an offence if—
   (a) he intentionally penetrates the vagina, anus or mouth of another person (B) with his penis,
   (b) B does not consent to the penetration, and
   (c) A does not reasonably believe that B consents.

A person consents if they agree by choice, and have the freedom and capacity to make that choice (s. 74 of the Act)—any consent given must be 'true' consent, not simply a *submission* induced by fear or fraud. Therefore, if the person does not have any real choice in the matter, or the choice is not a genuine exercise of free will, then he/she has not 'consented'. Obtaining consent by fear or force would not be 'true consent' but if consent has been obtained by other means it does not automatically mean that the person consented (answer C is incorrect). ROE did consent to having sexual intercourse with HANRAHAN but her consent was given with the express condition that HANRAHAN would wear a condom—he did put on a condom but then took it off and this would amount to an offence of rape (answer A is incorrect). The question is closely associated to the case law decision in *Assange* v *Sweden* [2011] EWHC 2489 (Admin). In this case, the Divisional Court considered the situation in which A knew that B (the complainant) would only consent to sexual intercourse if he used a condom. The court rejected the view that the conclusive presumption in s. 76 of the Sexual Offences Act 2003 would apply (answer B is incorrect) and concluded that the issue of consent could be determined under s. 74 rather than s. 76 (correct answer D), and stated that it would be open to a jury to hold that if B had made it clear that she would only consent to sexual intercourse if A used a condom, then there would be no consent if, without B's consent, A did not use a condom or removed or tore the condom. A's conduct in having sexual intercourse without a condom in circumstances where B had made it clear that she would only have sexual intercourse if A did use a condom, would therefore amount to an offence.

Crime, paras 1.12.3 to 1.12.3.3

61. Answer **B** — There are a variety of reasons allowing a court to make a parenting order (e.g. a child safety order has been made in respect of the child), not just the fact that the child or young person in question has been convicted of an offence, making answer A incorrect (s. 8(1) of the Crime and Disorder Act 1998). A court does not have to bind GIBSON over, although if it does not, it will have to state in open court why that is the case (s. 376(4)(b) of the Sentencing Act 2020), making answer D incorrect. The recognisance can be imposed on the parent or guardian; the period of a recognisance under this section may not be more three years and must end before the offender reaches the age of 18 (s. 376(7)), making answer C incorrect. A parenting order lasts for a period not exceeding 12 months (correct answer B) (s. 8(4) of the Crime and Disorder Act 1998).

General Police Duties, paras 3.7.8.1 to 3.7.8.2

62. Answer **C** — A joint criminal enterprise exists where two (or more) people embark on the commission of an offence by one or both (or all) of them. It is a joint enterprise because all the parties have a common goal—that an offence will be committed. In this case, there is a 'joint enterprise' as GUNNEL and PLEYDEN have agreed to steal a car from a garage (an offence of burglary). As the parties to a joint enterprise share a combined purpose, each would be liable for the consequences of the actions of the other in the pursuit of their joint enterprise. This would indicate GUNNEL is liable for the injury to HENDERSON but that is not the case (answers A and B are incorrect). Where the actions of one party to the joint enterprise are a departure from what was agreed, what is described as 'parasitic accessory liability' (where GUNNEL would be liable for the injury to HENDERSON) will not apply (correct answer C). A good example is provided by the *Crime Manual* where two men (A and B) agree to carry out an offence of theft. During the course of the offence, the owner of the property subject of the offence appears and tries to prevent the offence taking place. Offender A produces a flick-knife and stabs the victim, causing grievous bodily harm. Offender B had no idea that offender A had a flick-knife and had never contemplated the use of violence during the theft offence. The actions of offender A are a departure from the nature and type of crime that was envisaged by offender B who did not know that A possessed a flick-knife; it is an act so fundamentally different from that originally contemplated by B that B is most unlikely to be liable for the injuries caused to the victim (*R v Anderson* [1966] 2 QB 110)—you can see how this example connects to the scenario in the MCQ. Answer D is incorrect as an accessory does not have to physically take part in an offence to be liable for it.

Crime, paras 1.2.8 to 1.2.8.2

63. Answer **B** — Answer C is incorrect as para. 11.1 of Code C states that following a decision to arrest a suspect, they must not be interviewed about the relevant offence except at a police station or other authorised place of detention, unless the consequent delay would be likely to:
(a) lead to:
  • interference with, or harm to, evidence connected with an offence;
  • interference with, or physical harm to, other people; or
  • serious loss of, or damage to, property;
(b) lead to alerting other people suspected of committing an offence but not yet arrested for it; or (c) hinder the recovery of property obtained in consequence of the commission of an offence.

Answers A and D are incorrect as a juvenile can be interviewed without an appropriate adult being present if an officer of superintendent rank or above considers that delaying the interview will lead to the consequences in para. 11.1(a) to (c), and is satisfied that the interview would not significantly harm the person's physical or mental state.

Evidence and Procedure, paras 2.8.3, 2.8.3.2

64. Answer **A** — Section 6(5) of the Road Traffic Act 1988 states that if an accident occurs owing to the presence of a motor vehicle on a road or other public place and a constable reasonably believes that the person was driving, attempting to drive or in charge of the vehicle at the time of the accident, then the officer can require the person to cooperate with one or more of the preliminary tests. There is no need, under s. 6(5), for the officer making the requirement to be in uniform, meaning that answer B is incorrect. The word 'accident' is interpreted widely and an incident where the only person injured was the driver of the motor vehicle or the only vehicle damaged was that motor vehicle would still be considered an 'accident', making answer C incorrect. If PC ASKEW made the requirement and CORK took and failed the preliminary breath test, he could not be arrested under s. 6D of the Road Traffic Act 1988. Section 6D provides a power of arrest but s. 6D(3) specifically forbids the arrest of a person whilst they are at a hospital as a patient, making answer D incorrect. PC ASKEW would be allowed to make the requirement for the provision of the preliminary breath test if the medical practitioner in immediate charge of CORK's case has been notified of the proposal to make the requirement and does not object to the requirement being made (s. 9(1) of the Road Traffic Act 1988), making A the correct answer.

General Police Duties, paras 3.22.4.3, 3.22.4.5, 3.22.6

65. Answer **B** — Section 46 of the Children Act 1989 states:

(1) Where a constable has reasonable cause to believe that a child would otherwise be likely to suffer significant harm, he may—
    (a) remove the child to suitable accommodation and keep him there; or
    (b) take such steps as are reasonable to ensure the child's removal from any hospital, or other place, in which he is then being accommodated is prevented.

A 'child' is someone who is under 18 years old (s. 105), so TOPHAM is classed as a 'child' and answer A is incorrect. There is no requirement for an 'authorising officer'—the power is available to a constable, making answer C incorrect. The 'designated officer' in a police protection matter has a number of duties to fulfil but the 'initiating officer' (PC CARRIGAN) and the 'designated officer' must not carry out the two separate roles, meaning that answer D is incorrect. The longest a child can spend in 'police protection' is 72 hours (correct answer B).

Crime, para. 1.13.4

66. Answer **D** — The Police and Criminal Evidence Act 1984, s. 32 states:

(1) A constable may search an arrested person, in any case where the person to be searched *has been arrested at a place other than a police station*, if the constable has reasonable grounds for believing that the arrested person may present a danger to himself or others.

(2) Subject to subsections (3) to (5) below, a constable shall also have power in any such case—

    (a) to search the arrested person for anything—

        (i) which he might use to assist him to escape from lawful custody; or

        (ii) which might be evidence relating to an offence; and

    (b) if the offence for which he has been arrested is an indictable offence, to enter and search any premises in which he was when arrested or immediately before he was arrested for evidence relating to the offence.

As FOGARTY was arrested at a police station, the power under s. 32 is not available to PC MARRI (correct answer D).

General Police Duties, para. 3.2.5.2

67. Answer **C** — Section 14 of the Modern Slavery Act 2015 provides for slavery and trafficking prevention orders (STPO) on conviction. Section 14(1) enables a court (e.g. the magistrates' court, youth court, Crown Court or, in limited cases, the Court of Appeal) to impose a STPO on a person on a conviction or other finding in respect of that person for a slavery or human trafficking offence (answers B and D are incorrect). Answer A is incorrect as an STPO may last for a fixed period of at least five years or until further order (s. 17(4)). A STPO may prohibit a person from travelling to any specified country outside the United Kingdom, any country other than a country specified in the order or any country outside the United Kingdom (s. 18(2)) (correct answer C).

Crime, paras 1.11.4.7, 1.11.4.10

68. Answer **A** — Section 51A(1) of the Sexual Offences Act 2003 states that it is an offence for a person in a street or public place to solicit another (B) for the purpose of obtaining B's sexual services as a prostitute. The fact that the person solicited is not a prostitute is irrelevant, making answer D incorrect. Section 51A(2) states that the reference to a person in a street or public place includes a person in a vehicle in a street or public place. As 'kerb-crawling' or soliciting is punishable on the *first occasion* the activity takes place, this would mean that the offence is committed when MOSS solicits DOWELL when MOSS is inside his car (correct answer A) and that answer C is incorrect. In the case of 'kerb-crawling', there is no requirement for the soliciting to be shown to be likely to cause nuisance or annoyance to others, meaning that answer B is incorrect.

Crime, para. 1.12.15.5

69. Answer **D** — The Bail Act 1976, s. 7 states:

(3) A person who has been released on bail in criminal proceedings and is under a duty to surrender into the custody of a court may be arrested without warrant by a constable—

    (a) if the constable has reasonable grounds for believing that person is not likely to surrender to custody;

    (b) if the constable has reasonable grounds for believing that that person is likely to break any of the conditions of his bail or has reasonable grounds for suspecting that that person has broken any of those conditions; or

    (c) in a case where that person was released on bail with one or more surety or sureties, if a surety notifies a constable in writing that that person is unlikely to surrender to custody and that for that reason the surety wishes to be relieved of his obligations as a surety.

So PC LOW was correct to arrest ZHONG (as per s. 7(3)(c)), making answer A incorrect. Answer B is incorrect as s. 7 does not create an offence, it merely confers a power of arrest (*R v Gangar* [2008] EWCA Crim 2987). Answer C is incorrect as where a person is arrested under s. 7, he/she shall be brought before a magistrate as soon as practicable and in any event within 24 hours (s. 7(4)(a))—correct answer D. However, in the case of a person charged with murder, or with murder and one or more other offences, he/she must be brought before a judge of the Crown Court (s. 7(8)). This section requires that a detainee not merely be brought to the court precincts or cells but actually be dealt with by a justice within 24 hours of being arrested (*R (On the application of Culley) v Dorchester Crown Court* [2007] EWHC 109 (Admin)).

Evidence and Procedure, para. 2.2.9

70. Answer **A** — It seems that, apart from the offences of murder, attempted murder, treason and offences under the Misuse of Drugs Act 1971, the defence is available against any other charge (including hijacking, *R v Abdul-Hussain* [1999] Crim LR 570), making answers B and C incorrect. Answer D is incorrect as the defence of 'duress of circumstances' (necessity) is only available when the crime is committed in order to avoid death or serious injury—here ROSS is not committing the crime to avoid that outcome (ROSS is the victim of blackmail, of course, but you are not being questioned on that offence or the possible outcomes that these circumstances would have in reality—the question is asking about duress of circumstances and nothing else).

Crime, para. 1.4.4

71. Answer **A** — Under s. 165A of the Road Traffic Act 1988, a police officer has the power to seize a vehicle if he/she has reasonable grounds for believing that the driver does not have a suitable licence or that the vehicle is not adequately insured. To seize a vehicle, a police officer must be in uniform and have requested to see the relevant documents. He/she must also warn the driver that the vehicle will be seized unless the documents are produced immediately (however, if it is impractical to warn the driver then a warning is not required (s. 165A(6))). If the driver has failed to stop or has driven off, the vehicle may be seized at any time in the 24-hour period following the incident (making answers B and D incorrect as the vehicle cannot be seized). A police officer has the legal power to enter premises to seize a vehicle, including from a driveway or garage associated with a private dwelling-house (answer C is incorrect). The officer must have reasonable grounds for believing the vehicle to be present, and reasonable force may be used if necessary.

General Police Duties, para. 3.20.6

72. Answer **C** — A confession is defined by s. 82(1) of the Police and Criminal Evidence Act 1984 as a 'statement wholly or partly adverse to the person who made it, whether made to a person in authority or not and whether made in words or otherwise'. This means that the response to the question asked by ARTHERN and the statement to PC EDDOWES would be confessions (answers A, B and D are incorrect).

Evidence and Procedure, para. 2.4.2

73. Answer **A** — Section 1A of the Sporting Events (Control of Alcohol etc.) Act 1985 states:

(1) This section applies to a motor vehicle which—
  (a) is not a public service vehicle but is adapted to carry more than 8 passengers, and
  (b) is being used for the principal purpose of carrying two or more passengers for the whole or part of a journey to or from a designated sporting event.
(2) A person who knowingly causes or permits alcohol to be carried on a motor vehicle to which this section applies is guilty of an offence—
  (a) if he is its driver, or
  (b) if he is not its driver but is its keeper, the servant or agent of its keeper, a person to whom it is made available (by hire, loan or otherwise) by its keeper or the keeper's servant or agent, or the servant or agent of a person to whom it is so made available.
(3) A person who has alcohol in his possession while on a motor vehicle to which this section applies is guilty of an offence.
(4) A person who is drunk on a motor vehicle to which this section applies is guilty of an offence.

If the vehicle in question was adapted to carry more than eight passengers, then all three of the named individuals would commit the offence—but it is only adapted to carry six passengers and the driver so the s. 1A offence would not apply to the vehicle and occupants, meaning that answers B, C and D are incorrect.

General Police Duties, para. 3.10.5.2

74. Answer **B** — The Theft Act 1968, s. 24A states:

(1) A person is guilty of an offence if—
  (a) a wrongful credit has been made to an account kept by him or in respect of which he has any right or interest;
  (b) he knows or believes that the credit is wrongful; and
  (c) he dishonestly fails to take such steps as are reasonable in the circumstances to secure that the credit is cancelled.
(2) References to a credit are to a credit of an amount of money.

The offence is committed when GARNER retains the wrongful credit (correct answer B). Section 24A(2A) states that a credit to an account is 'wrongful' if it derives from theft, blackmail or fraud (under s. 1 of the Fraud Act 2006), making answers A and C incorrect. Answer D is incorrect as s. 24A(5) states that in determining whether a credit to an account is wrongful, it is immaterial (in particular) whether the account is overdrawn before or after the credit is made.

Crime, para. 1.14.12

75. Answer **A** — Answers C and D are incorrect. In *R* v *B* [2006] EWCA Crim 2945, the Court of Appeal stated that whether an individual had a sexual disease or condition, such as being HIV-positive, was not an issue as far as consent was concerned. The case related to a man who was alleged to have raped a woman after they had met outside a nightclub. When arrested, the man informed the custody officer that he was HIV-positive, a fact he had not disclosed to the victim prior to sexual intercourse. At the original trial, the judge directed that this non-disclosure was relevant to the issue of consent. On appeal, the court stated that this

was not the case and that the consent issue for a jury to consider was whether or not the victim consented to sexual intercourse, not whether she consented to sexual intercourse with a person suffering from a sexually transmitted disease. However, in *R v McNally* [2013] EWCA Crim 1051 the Court of Appeal observed that *B* was not an authority that HIV status *could not* vitiate consent. *B* left the issue open and HIV status *could* vitiate consent if, for example, the complainant had been positively assured that the accused was not HIV-positive. However, in this MCQ such a positive assurance does not play any part in the scenario—CHESTERFIELD never mentioned his HIV status and the fact that he wore a condom does not have any impact in relation to this set of circumstances when considering the offence of rape; he would not commit that offence. However, the courts have recognised that person-to-person transmission of a sexual infection that will have serious consequences for the infected person's health can amount to grievous bodily harm under the Offences Against the Person Act 1861 (in *R v Dica* [2004] EWCA Crim 1103 there was an acceptance that the *deliberate* infection of another with the HIV virus could amount to grievous bodily harm). This issue was explored further in *R v Konzani* [2005] EWCA Crim 706. In that case, the defendant appealed against convictions for inflicting grievous bodily harm on three women contrary to s. 20. The defendant had unprotected consensual sexual intercourse with the women but *without having disclosed* that he was HIV-positive. The women subsequently contracted the HIV virus. The Court of Appeal held that there was a critical distinction between taking a risk as to the various potentially adverse (and possibly problematic) consequences of unprotected consensual intercourse, and the giving of informed consent to the risk of infection with a fatal disease. Answer D is incorrect as the circumstances of this MCQ mean that CHESTERFIELD would commit a s. 20 offence (correct answer A).

Crime, paras 1.10.7.4, 1.12.3 to 1.12.3.1

76. Answer **D** — The first thing to consider here is Code E of the Codes of Practice. Para. 1.13 states:

Nothing in this Code requires the identity of officers or police staff conducting interviews to be recorded or disclosed if the interviewer reasonably believes recording or disclosing their name might put them in danger. In these cases, the officers and staff should use warrant or other identification numbers and the name of their police station. Such instances and the reasons for them shall be recorded in the custody record or the interviewer's pocket book.

This is relevant to visually recorded interviews where, at para. 2.7 of Code F we are told that:

In cases to which paragraph 1.13 of Code E (disclosure of identity of officers or police staff conducting interviews) applies:

(a) the officers and staff may have their backs to the visual recording device; and
(b) when in accordance with Code E paragraph 3.21 or 4.12 as they apply to this Code, arrangements are made for the suspect to have access to the visual recording, the investigating officer may arrange for anything in the recording that might allow the officers or police staff to be identified to be concealed.

Therefore answer D is correct and answers A, B and C are incorrect.

Evidence and Procedure, paras 2.8.7, 2.8.13

77. Answer **A** — The Criminal Attempts Act 1981, s. 1 states:

(1) If, with intent to commit an offence to which this section applies, a person does an act which is more than merely preparatory to the commission of the offence, he is guilty of attempting to commit the offence.

(2) A person may be guilty of attempting to commit an offence to which this section applies even though the facts are such that the commission of the offence is impossible.

(3) In any case where—
  (a) apart from this subsection a person's intention would not be regarded as having amounted to an intent to commit an offence; but
  (b) if the facts of the case had been as he believed them to be, his intention would be so regarded, then, for the purposes of subsection (1) above, he shall be regarded as having had an intent to commit that offence.

To prove an 'attempt', you must show an *intention* on the part of the defendant to commit the substantive offence. This requirement means a higher level or degree of *mens rea* may be required to prove an attempt than for the substantive offence. For instance, the *mens rea* required to prove an offence of murder is the intention to kill *or* cause grievous bodily harm whereas the *mens rea* for attempted murder is nothing less than an *intent* to kill (*R v Whybrow* (1951) 35 Cr App R 141). DARLOW does not have the *mens rea* required to commit this offence (the intention to kill), making answer A correct and answers C and D incorrect. Answer B is incorrect as the fact that it would be impossible for DARLOW to throw acid over the pair would not preclude an attempted murder charge if he had the correct *mens rea*.

Crime, para. 1.3.4

78. Answer **A** — The Serious Crime Act 2007, s. 44 states:

(1) A person commits an offence if—
  (a) he does an act capable of encouraging or assisting in the commission of an offence; and
  (b) he intends to encourage or assist its commission.

(2) But he is not to be taken to have intended to encourage or assist the commission of an offence merely because such encouragement or assistance was a foreseeable consequence of his act.

Section 51 limits the liability of the offence by setting out in statute the exception established in the case *R v Tyrrell* [1894] 1 QB 710. Therefore a person cannot be guilty under ss. 44, 45 and 46 of this Act; that is a 'protective' offence, making A the correct answer as FIELD was encouraging an offence that is for her own protection.

Crime, para. 1.3.2

79. Answer **B** — Under s. 1 of the Children and Young Persons Act 1933, an offence is committed when the offender 'neglects' a child. A person will be presumed to have neglected the child where it is proved that the child was an infant under 3 years old who died as a result of suffocation (other than by disease or blockage of the airways by an object) while in bed with someone of 16 years or over who was under the influence of drink or a prohibited drug when he/she went to bed or at any later time before the suffocation (s. 1(2)(b)). A drug is a prohibited drug for the purpose of s. 1(2)(b) in relation to a person if the person's possession of the drug

immediately before taking it constituted an offence under s. 5(2) of the Misuse of Drugs Act 1971. This makes answers C and D incorrect.

Answer A is incorrect as the reference in s. 1(2)(b) to the infant being 'in bed' with another ('the adult') includes a reference to the infant lying next to the adult in or on any kind of furniture or surface being used by the adult for the purpose of sleeping (and the reference to the time when the adult 'went to bed' is to be read accordingly) (s. 1(2A)). A defendant may be charged with the above offence even where the child has died (s. 1(3)(b)) (correct answer B).

Crime, para. 1.13.3

80. Answer **D** — The Road Traffic Act 1988, s. 6D states:

(1) A constable may arrest a person without warrant if as a result of a preliminary breath test or preliminary drug test the constable reasonably suspects that—
   (a) the proportion of alcohol in the person's breath or blood exceeds the prescribed limit, or
   (b) the person has a specified controlled drug in his body and the proportion of it in the person's blood or urine exceeds the specified limit for that drug.
(1A) ...
(2) A constable may arrest a person without warrant if—
   (a) the person fails to co-operate with a preliminary test in pursuance of a requirement imposed under section 6, and
   (b) the constable reasonably suspects that the person has alcohol or a drug in his body or is under the influence of a drug.

The powers of arrest are available to a constable (in uniform or not) making answer A incorrect. The powers under s. 6D are not limited to situations where the offence has taken place on a road, making answer B incorrect. Suspicion that KENYON is under the influence of a drug might well generate preliminary test powers or even allow the officer to arrest a person for being unfit (s. 4 of the Act) but suspicion alone does not provide the grounds to arrest a person under s. 6D, making answer C incorrect. If KENYON had taken and failed a preliminary test, an arrest could be made under s. 6D—that arrest could also take place if KENYON failed to cooperate with a preliminary test and the officer suspected that he had a drug in his body or was under the influence of a drug (correct answer D).

General Police Duties, para. 3.22.4.5

81. Answer **D** — The first point to make is that DUFFY has committed an offence under s. 4(1) of the Road Traffic Act 1988 (driving whilst unfit). Section 4 of the Act states that a person who, when driving or attempting to drive a mechanically propelled vehicle on a road or other public place, is unfit to drive through drink or drugs is guilty of an offence. DC STAMP would be entitled to arrest DUFFY in these circumstances, meaning that answer A is incorrect. Breaking the arm of the officer is a serious injury amounting to grievous bodily harm (according to the CPS charging standards), meaning that answer B is incorrect. Although DUFFY did not intend to injure the officer in this way, this is still a s. 18 offence. Section 18 wounding/GBH is committed when a person *unlawfully and maliciously* by any means whatsoever wounds or causes any grievous bodily harm to any person with intent to do some grievous bodily harm to any person,

or with intent to resist or prevent the lawful apprehension or detainer of any person. It is the latter element that would cover DUFFY's behaviour as this is a form of the s. 18 offence. In these circumstances, DUFFY has maliciously caused grievous bodily harm to the officer with intent to resist or prevent the lawful apprehension etc. of any person. Here 'maliciously' means that the person must be subjectively reckless in relation to a risk of harm—DUFFY realises there is a risk of harm so that element is satisfied. The activity was carried out with intent to resist arrest so this is a s. 18 offence, meaning that answer C is incorrect.

EXCLUDED QUESTION, *Crime*, paras 1.10.7.3 to 1.10.7.5

82. Answer **A** — The offence of violent disorder has been committed by all three men in this scenario. The fact that the three men did not act deliberately in combination with each other does not matter as the Court of Appeal has held that for the purposes of this section it was not necessary for a person to act deliberately in combination with at least two others present at the scene, but that it is sufficient that at least three people are present, each separately using or threatening unlawful violence (*R* v *NW* [2010] EWCA Crim 404), making answer B incorrect. The offence can be committed by using or threatening violence so HARLOW's conduct would be caught. The fact that the violence used by GREEN was towards property does not mean anything when considering violent disorder (it is only s. 3 affray where this plays a part), so answers C and D are incorrect.

General Police Duties, para. 3.9.4

83. Answer **B** — The Firearms Act 1968, s. 19 states:

A person commits an offence if, without lawful authority or reasonable excuse (the proof whereof lies on him), he has with him in a public place—

(a) a loaded shot gun,
(b) an air weapon (whether loaded or not),
(c) any other firearm (whether loaded or not) together with ammunition suitable for use in that firearm, or
(d) an imitation firearm.

An 'airsoft gun' is not to be regarded as a firearm for the purposes of this Act (s. 57A(1)). Section 57A(2) states that an 'airsoft gun' is a barrelled weapon of any description which:

• is designed to discharge only a small plastic missile (whether or not it is also capable of discharging any other kind of missile); and
• is not capable of discharging a missile (of any kind) with kinetic energy at the muzzle of the weapon that exceeds the permitted level.

A 'small plastic missile' is a missile made wholly or partly from plastics, is spherical and does not exceed 8 mm in diameter (s. 57A(3)).

The exemption is not absolute—if the kinetic energy at the muzzle exceeds the permitted level, then it will be a firearm. The 'permitted kinetic energy level' is:

• in the case of a weapon which is capable of discharging two or more missiles successively without repeated pressure on the trigger (an automatic weapon), 1.3 joules;
• in any other case (a single shot variant), 2.5 joules.

As the airsoft gun is a single shot variant with a kinetic energy level of 1.34 joules, it is not a firearm and possession of it is not an offence which makes answer A incorrect. Answer C is incorrect as the definition of a firearm under s. 57(1) of the Firearms Act 1968 does not include telescopic sights or magazines. Answer D is incorrect as a 'public place' includes any highway and any other premises or place to which, at the material time, the public have or are permitted to have access whether on payment or otherwise (s. 57(4) of the Act)—that would certainly include the showground MAXWELL was searched in.

Crime, paras 1.7.2, 1.7.10.1

84. Answer **B** — Annex B of Code D (para. 9) states that an identification parade shall consist of at least eight people (in addition to the suspect) who, so far as possible, resemble the suspect in age, height, general appearance and position in life. Only one suspect shall be included in an identification parade *unless there are two suspects of roughly similar appearance, in which case they may be paraded together with at least 12 other people* (correct answer B). So the parade can take place (making answer A incorrect) and will be with at least 12 other people (making answer D incorrect). There is no requirement for certification that such a procedure should take place because of expediency (answer C is incorrect).

Evidence and Procedure, para. 2.7.9

85. Answer **C** — The Sexual Offences Act 2003, s. 66 states:

(1) A person commits an offence if—
    (a) he intentionally exposes his genitals, and
    (b) he intends that someone will see them and be caused alarm or distress.

The offence can be committed in public or private and there is no requirement that the defendant acts for the purposes of sexual gratification, making answer A incorrect. The offence only applies to the genitals, not the buttocks, so the act of 'mooning' will not be covered, making answer B incorrect. A woman who exposes her breasts will not be guilty of an offence under s. 66, making answer D incorrect. If the genitals are not exposed for the relevant reason, the offence is not committed (correct answer C).

Crime, para. 1.12.18.1

86. Answer **B** — The initial period for a s. 60AA authorisation can last a maximum of 24 hours, making answer A incorrect. There is no power to stop and search persons and/or vehicles attached to a s. 60AA authorisation, making answer C incorrect. Once the initial authorisation period has ended, the power can be extended for a further 24 hours by an officer of the rank of superintendent or above, making answer D incorrect.

General Police Duties, paras 3.1.4.8 to 3.1.4.9

87. Answer **C** — A misconduct meeting shall take place not later than 20 working days beginning with the first working day after the date on which the documents and material for the meeting were supplied to the police officer under reg. 30 of the Police (Conduct) Regulations 2020. The person conducting or chairing the misconduct proceedings may extend the time limit where they consider that this would be in the interests of justice.

General Police Duties, para. 3.17.6.1

88. Answer **A** — The Road Traffic Act 1988, s. 6 states:

(1) If any of subsections (2) to (5) applies a constable may require a person to co-operate with any one or more preliminary tests administered to the person by that constable or another constable.

(2) This subsection applies if a constable reasonably suspects that the person—
   (a) is driving, is attempting to drive or is in charge of a motor vehicle on a road or other public place, and
   (b) has alcohol or a drug in his body or is under the influence of a drug.

(3) This subsection applies if a constable reasonably suspects that the person—
   (a) has been driving, attempting to drive or in charge of a motor vehicle on a road or other public place while having alcohol or a drug in his body or while unfit to drive because of a drug, and
   (b) still has alcohol or a drug in his body or is still under the influence of a drug.

(4) This subsection applies if a constable reasonably suspects that the person—

   (a) is or has been driving, attempting to drive or in charge of a motor vehicle on a road or other public place, and
   (b) has committed a traffic offence while the vehicle was in motion.

PC PLATTEN can require GREY to cooperate with a preliminary test under s. 6(3) so the correct answer is A. The administration of the test in such a situation would be by an officer in uniform but the officer making the requirement can be in plain clothes or uniform so answer C is incorrect. The facts that this is not a reportable accident and that nobody has been injured are irrelevant, making answers B and D incorrect.

General Police Duties, para. 3.22.4

89. Answer **D** — A common assault by battery (beating) involves the actual use of force by an assailant on a victim but which only results in very minor or no perceivable injury. It is the intentional or reckless application of force on another and can range from a push to a punch, and depends on how much harm is done and the injury received. The application of force can be carried out indirectly—the circumstances of the question are such an example where injury is caused to the baby by BOTHAM punching ZAPPE who drops the baby to the ground causing slight injury. This is a s. 39 offence (a battery) meaning that answers B and C are eliminated. The offence under s. 47 of the Offences Against the Person Act 1861 (Actual Bodily Harm (ABH)) is exactly the same as a s. 39 offence but can be distinguished from a s. 39 by the degree of injury. *R v Donovan* [1934] 2 KB 498 at 509, [1934] All ER Rep 207 suggested that 'bodily harm has its ordinary meaning' and includes 'any hurt or injury calculated to interfere with the health or comfort of the victim. Such hurt or injury need not be permanent, but must, no doubt, be more than merely transient and trifling.' A momentary loss of consciousness has been held to be 'actual harm' (*R v Miller*; *T v DPP* [2003] EWHC 266 (Admin))—the significant bruising is just that, 'significant', and amounts to more than transient/trifling harm (ABH) therefore a charge of s. 47 would be appropriate in this situation, making answer A incorrect.

Crime, paras 1.10.3, 1.10.7.1, 1.10.7.3

90. Answer **C** — Answer A is incorrect as a road check under s. 4 of the Police and Criminal Evidence Act 1984 can be authorised for a number of reasons. Section 4(1) states:

(1) This section shall have effect in relation to the conduct of road checks by police officers for the purpose of ascertaining whether a vehicle is carrying—
   (a) a person who has committed an offence other than a road traffic offence or a vehicle excise offence;
   (b) a person who is a witness to such an offence;
   (c) a person intending to commit such an offence; or
   (d) a person who is unlawfully at large.

It is correct that a road check should be authorised in writing and if authorised will last for a period of seven days; however, answers B and D are incorrect as a road check will be authorised by an officer of superintendent rank or above.

General Police Duties, para. 3.20.3

91. Answer **C** — PACE, s. 61A, provides power for a police officer to take footwear impressions without consent from any person over the age of 10 years who is detained at a police station:

(a) in consequence of being arrested for a recordable offence; or if the detainee has been charged with a recordable offence, or informed they will be reported for such an of-fence; and
(b) the detainee has not had an impression of their footwear taken in the course of the in-vestigation of the offence unless the previously taken impression is not complete or is not of sufficient quality to allow satisfactory analysis, comparison or matching (whether in the case in question or generally).

Answer C is correct as no consent is required (answers A and B are incorrect in that regard) and the footwear impressions can be taken (answer D is incorrect).

Evidence and Procedure, para. 2.7.5.3

92. Answer **B** — Section 30 of the Police and Criminal Evidence Act 1984 provides for the procedure to be adopted after a person has been arrested. Section 30 states:

(1) Subsection (1A) applies where a person is, at any place other than a police station—
   (a) arrested by a constable for an offence, or
   (b) taken into custody by a constable after being arrested for an offence by a person other than a constable.
(1A) The person must be taken by a constable to a *police station* as soon as practicable after the arrest.

So PACE requires that such an arrested person be taken to a *police station*. Section 30(2) states that subject to subss. (3) and (5) of s. 30, the police station to which an arrested person is taken under subs. (1A) above shall be a *designated police station*. However, as there are exceptions to this requirement contained in s. 30(3) and (5), answer A must be incorrect.

Section 30(5) states that any constable may take an arrested person to any police station if:

(a) either of the following conditions is satisfied—
    (i) the constable has arrested him without the assistance of any other constable and no other constable is available to assist him;
    (ii) the constable has taken him into custody from a person other than a constable without the assistance of any other constable and no other constable is available to assist him; and
(b) it appears to the constable that he will be unable to take the arrested person to a designated police station without the arrested person injuring himself, the constable or some other person.

The behaviour of PC CURTIS would be covered by s. 30(5)(a)(i) and (b) so her behaviour is lawful, making answer C incorrect.

Section 30(6) states that if the first police station to which an arrested person is taken after their arrest is not a designated police station, he/she shall be taken to a designated police station not more than six hours after their arrival at the first police station unless he/she is released previously (correct answer B). There is no requirement to contact an inspector and transport the arrested person as soon as practicable as mentioned in the incorrect answer D.

General Police Duties, para. 3.3.12

93. Answer **A** — Section 27 of the Theft Act 1968 allows for the admissibility of previous misconduct and states:

(3) Where a person is being proceeded against for handling stolen goods (but not for any offence other than handling stolen goods), then at any stage of the proceedings, if evidence has been given of his having or arranging to have in his possession the goods the subject of the charge, or of his undertaking or assisting in, or arranging to undertake or assist in, their retention, removal, disposal or realisation, the following evidence shall be admissible for the purpose of proving that he knew or believed the goods to be stolen goods—
    (a) evidence that he has had in his possession, or has undertaken or assisted in the retention, removal, disposal or realisation of, stolen goods from any theft taking place not earlier than 12 months before the offence charged; and
    (b) (provided that seven days' notice in writing has been given to him of the intention to prove the conviction) evidence that he has within the five years preceding the date of the offence charged been convicted of theft or of handling stolen goods.

Therefore DUBAR's previous conviction and the evidence that he had stolen property in his possession nine months before the handling offence he is charged with are admissible, making answers B, C and D incorrect.

Crime, para. 1.14.11.4

94. Answer **C** — There are a number of reasons that an interview may be recorded in writing. Code E, para. 2.3 states that a written record of the matters described in para. 2.1(a) and (b) shall be made in accordance with Code C, s. 11 if an authorised recording device in working order is not available (that is the case in this scenario) and (c) the 'relevant officer' described in para. 2.4 considers, on reasonable grounds, that the proposed interview or (as the case may be) continuation of the interview or other action, should not be delayed until an authorised recording device in working order and a suitable interview room or other location become available and decides that a written

record shall be made. Paragraph 2.4(c)(i) states that in the case of a voluntary interview which takes place at a police station and the offence in question is an indictable offence, the 'relevant officer' means an officer of the rank of sergeant or above, in consultation with the investigating officer—therefore the answer is C and answers A, B and D are incorrect.

Evidence and Procedure, para. 2.8.8

95. Answer **D** — The 'relevant time' of a person's detention starts in accordance with s. 41(2)–(5) of the Police and Criminal Evidence Act 1984. The time from which the period of detention of a person is to be calculated (in this Act referred to as 'the relevant time') will be in the case of a person arrested outside England and Wales, the time at which that person arrives at the first police station to which he/she is taken in the police area in England or Wales in which the offence for which he/she was arrested is being investigated (17.30hrs Wednesday) or the time 24 hours after the time of that person's entry into England and Wales whichever is the earlier.

Evidence and Procedure, para. 2.6.16.1

96. Answer **D** — Answer D is correct as this legislation covers the offence of common assault, or battery, when committed against an emergency worker acting in the exercise of functions as such a worker (including when an emergency worker is not at work but is carrying out the same activities as he/she would do at work).

Crime, para. 1.10.7.2

97. Answer **B** — Answer A is incorrect as people who have a disability, *or have had a disability in the past*, are protected against discrimination. Answer C is incorrect as people who are not married or civil partners do not have this characteristic but the Marriage (Same Sex Couples) Act 2013 extended marriage to same-sex couples and the Civil Partnership (Opposite-sex Couples) Regulations 2019 extended civil partnership to opposite-sex couples (they do have this characteristic). Answer D is incorrect as 'ethnic group' may include any group with a shared culture or history (*Mandla v Dowell Lee* [1983] 2 AC 548). Sikhs (*Mandla v Dowell Lee* [1983] 2 AC 548), Jewish people (*Seide v Gillette Industries Ltd* [1980] IRLR 427), Romany Gypsies (*Commission for Racial Equality v Dutton* [1989] QB 783) and Irish Travellers (*O'Leary v Allied Domecq Inns Ltd* (CL 950275 July 2000, Central London County Court) have all been held to be ethnic groups, but Scots, Welsh and English are however **not** ethnic groups (*Dawkins v Department of the Environment* [1993] IRLR 284). Answer B is therefore the correct answer. Section 10(2) of the Equality Act 2010 (Religion and Belief) states that belief means any religious or philosophical belief and a reference to belief includes a reference to a lack of belief. The criteria for determining what is a 'philosophical belief' are that it must be genuinely held; be a belief and not an opinion or viewpoint based on the present state of information available; be a belief as to a weighty and substantial aspect of human life and behaviour; attain a certain level of cogency, seriousness, cohesion and importance; and be worthy of respect in a democratic society, compatible with human dignity and not conflict with the fundamental rights of others. For example, a belief in 'climate change' affecting how a person lived his/her life is protected by the Act (*Grainger plc v Nicholson* [2010] 2 All ER 253). A philosophical belief would only be excluded for failing to satisfy *Grainger plc* if it was the kind of belief the expression of which would be akin to Nazism or totalitarianism. The claimant held gender-critical beliefs, which included the belief that sex is immutable and not to be conflated with gender identity. Some transgender people found the claimant's remarks offensive and 'transphobic'. The tribunal held that the complainant's beliefs were widely shared and did not seek to destroy

the rights of trans persons. The claimant's belief, whilst offensive to some, and notwithstanding its potential to result in the harassment of trans persons in some circumstances, fell within the protection under Article 9 of the ECHR and therefore was in line with s. 10 of the Equality Act 2010 (*Forstater v CGD Europe* [2021] UKEAT 0105 20 1006).

General Police Duties, paras 3.16.3.2, 3.16.3.4 to 3.16.3.6

98. Answer **C** — The Licensing Act 1872, s. 12 states:

Every person found drunk in any highway or other public place, whether a building or not, or on any licensed premises, shall be liable …

The offence is not limited to being found drunk on licensed premises, meaning that answer D is incorrect. It includes being found drunk 'on any licensed premises' meaning that answer B is incorrect. The offence has been held to apply to a licensee when found drunk on the licensed premises, even when those premises were not open to the public (*Evans* v *Fletcher* (1926) 135 LT 153) so both men commit the offence (correct answer C) and this means that answer A is incorrect.

General Police Duties, para. 3.6.9

99. Answer **C** — Recklessness is a state of mind that is relevant to a large number of crimes and is essentially concerned with unjustified risk-taking. Answer B is wrong as following the case of *R v G and R* [2003] UKHL 50, the approach taken to the interpretation of the word 'reckless' is that it will be 'subjective' and does not involve a 'reasonable bystander' test (which would effectively make the test 'objective').

The requirements of subjective recklessness can be found in the case of *R* v *Cunningham* [1957] 2 QB 396 and are satisfied in situations where *the defendant* foresees the consequences of his/her actions as being probable or even possible. In *G*, the House of Lords held that a person acts recklessly with respect to:

- a circumstance when he/she is *aware* of a risk that it exists or will exist;
- a result when he/she is *aware* of the risk that it will occur;

and it is, in the circumstances known to him/her, *unreasonable* to take that risk.

To establish recklessness therefore requires consideration of the degree of risk that is actually foreseen by the defendant of which he/she is aware and whether it was reasonable. Answer D is incorrect as whilst the risk a defendant is aware of may be small that does not automatically mean that it is reasonable to take that risk. Each situation will be decided on its own merits but whether the risk is reasonable or not will be decided by the court—not the defendant. What this does is to introduce an objective element into the recklessness equation but, even though that is the case, it must be stressed that recklessness is still subjective—the key question is whether the defendant was aware of the risk.

Depending on the crime, the nature of the risk the defendant needs to be aware of will change. For example, to commit an offence under s. 20 of the Offences Against the Person Act 1861 (wounding or inflicting grievous bodily harm (see *Crime Manual*, chapter 1.10)), the defendant must unlawfully and recklessly wound or inflict grievous bodily harm on the victim. Here 'recklessness' means that the defendant was aware of the risk that *some harm* would befall the victim, making answer A incorrect and answer C correct.

Crime, paras 1.1.3 to 1.1.3.3

100. Answer **A** — Code D, para. 3.11 states that no officer or any other person involved with the investigation of the case against the suspect may take any part in those procedures or act as the identification officer, meaning that answers C and D are incorrect. Paragraph 3.11 also states that arrangements for, and conduct of, the eye-witness identification procedures in paras 3.5 to 3.10 and circumstances in which any such identification procedure must be held shall be the responsibility of an officer not below inspector rank who is not involved with the investigation ('the identification officer'). This would appear to mean that answer B is correct; however, para. 3.19 states that in the case of a detained suspect, the duties under paras 3.17 and 3.18 (providing an explanation of the identification procedure and the notice in relation to it) may be performed by the custody officer or by another officer or police staff not involved in the investigation as directed by the custody officer, if:

(a) it is proposed to release the suspect in order that an identification procedure can be arranged and carried out and an inspector is not available to act as the identification officer, before the suspect leaves the station; or
(b) it is proposed to keep the suspect in police detention whilst the procedure is arranged and carried out and waiting for an inspector to act as the identification officer would cause unreasonable delay to the investigation.

The officer concerned shall inform the identification officer of the action taken and give them the signed copy of the notice. Therefore answer A is the correct option.

Evidence and Procedure, para. 2.7.4.6

101. Answer **D** — Section 62A creates two situations in which the power to direct people to leave land can be exercised: *one excluding the element at s. 62(2)(d) and one including it.* The table below illustrates the relevant circumstances; in order for a direction to be given under s. 62A, the senior officer present at the scene must have a reasonable belief that:

Situation 1	Situation 2
at least two people are trespassing on the land; and	at least two people are trespassing on the land;
↓	↓
that they have at least one vehicle between them; and	that they have at least one vehicle between them; and
↓	↓
that they are there with the common purpose of residing there for any period; and	that they are there with the common purpose of residing there for any period; and
↓	↓
that the occupier (or person acting on the occupier's behalf) has asked the police to remove the trespassers from the land.	it appears to the officer that the person has one or more caravans in his possession or under his control on the land that there are relevant caravan sites with suitable pitches available for the trespassers to move to; and
	↓
	that the occupier (or person acting on the occupier's behalf) has asked the police to remove the trespassers from the land

HODGSON is the only person trespassing so a s. 62A direction could not be given in this situation (correct answer D).

General Police Duties, para. 3.5.5

102. Answer **C** — Under s. 89(2) of the Police Act 1996, it is an offence to *wilfully* obstruct a police officer or any person assisting the officer in the lawful execution of his/her duty (not accidentally—answer D is incorrect). It does not require an intentional or reckless element (answer A is incorrect). Answer B is incorrect as although obstruction can be committed by an omission to do something, that is only where a person was already obliged to undertake some duty for a police officer (and HALEEM would have no such obligation in this situation). The obstruction must be wilful—HALEEM may have accidentally made it harder for the officer to carry out his duty but that would not mean that he commits this offence.

Crime, para. 1.10.8.3

103. Answer **A** — A person who has anything in his/her custody or under his/her control intending without lawful excuse to use it or cause or permit another to use it:
    (a) to destroy or damage any property belonging to some other person; or
    (b) to destroy or damage his own or the user's property in a way which he knows is likely to endanger the life of some other person;

    shall be guilty of an offence under s. 3 of the Criminal Damage Act 1971. The offence can take place anywhere, making answer B incorrect. Possession of the relevant article is one of the ways the offence can be committed; it can also be committed if a person has custody or control over the article. The correct answer is A as EWER has custody of the shears as they are in her garden shed. The moment she decides to use them to commit criminal damage (custody + relevant intent), the offence is committed, making answers C and D incorrect.

Crime, para. 1.16.6

104. Answer **A** — Answer B is incorrect as in *R* v *Bannister* [2009] EWCA Crim 1571, the Court of Appeal ruled that an advanced police driver with highly developed driving skills was *not* entitled to have that ability taken into account when deciding whether or not the driving in question was dangerous. Answer C is incorrect as in *DPP* v *Harris* [1995] RTR 100, the Divisional Court held that the wording of the regulation meant that there was no scope for the defence of necessity where police drivers went through red traffic lights. Answer D is incorrect as if a person drives in a way that creates a need for police officers to pursue that person and an officer is subsequently injured in that pursuit, that person may owe a duty of care to the police officer and may therefore be sued for damages. In *Langley* v *Dray* [1997] PIQR P508 (confirmed by the Court of Appeal [1998] PIQR P314), the court held that the driver of the stolen motor vehicle owed a duty of care to the police officer pursuing him. He knew or ought to have known that the police were in pursuit and should not have gone so fast while driving on ice. He had a duty not to create such a risk. Answer A is correct as while the particular circumstances under which the police driver was driving may not provide a specific defence, they may nevertheless provide mitigation and, where appropriate, special reasons for not disqualifying the driver (see e.g. *Agnew* v *DPP* [1991] RTR 144).

General Police Duties, para. 3.19.13.3

105. Answer **C** — There is no specific provision within the Police and Criminal Evidence Act 1984 or the Codes of Practice for the disclosure of any information by the police at the police station, *with the exception of the custody record* (so the custody record must be disclosed, making answers A and B incorrect). In respect of the provision of a copy of the 'first description' of a suspect, it should be noted that Code D (para. 3.1) states that a copy of the 'first description' shall, where practicable, be given to the suspect or his/her solicitor before any procedures under paras 3.5 to 3.10, 3.21 or 3.23 are carried out. In other words, the disclosure requirement is that a copy of the 'first description' shall, where practicable, be given to the suspect or his/her solicitor before a video identification, an identification parade, a group identification or confrontation takes place. Therefore, an officer disclosing information to a solicitor at the interview stage (which is taking place in advance of any identification procedures) need not provide the 'first description' of a suspect at that time.

Further, there is nothing within the Criminal Justice and Public Order Act 1994 that states that information must be disclosed before an inference from silence can be made (making answer D incorrect).

Evidence and Procedure, para. 2.8.4.3

106. Answer **C** — The Police and Criminal Evidence Act 1984, s. 19 states:

(1) The powers conferred by subsections (2), (3) and (4) below are exercisable by a constable who is lawfully on any premises.
(2) The constable may seize anything which is on the premises if he has reasonable grounds for believing—
   (a) that it has been obtained in consequence of the commission of an offence; and
   (b) that it is necessary to seize it in order to prevent it being concealed, lost, damaged, altered or destroyed.
(3) The constable may seize anything which is on the premises if he has reasonable grounds for believing—
   (a) that it is evidence in relation to an offence which he is investigating or any other offence; and
   (b) that it is necessary to seize it in order to prevent the evidence being concealed, lost, altered or destroyed.

Answer D is incorrect as s. 19 is a power of seizure, not a power of entry. For this power to apply, the officers concerned must be on the premises lawfully. If the officers are on the premises only with the consent of the occupier, they become trespassers once that consent has been withdrawn (as it has been in this set of circumstances). Once the officers are told to leave, they are no longer 'lawfully' on the premises. They must be given a reasonable opportunity to leave and *cannot then seize any property that they may find*. So DC JAMES could not seize the watch and answer B is incorrect. Even if DC JAMES 'believed' rather than suspected that the watch was stolen, that would not change the fact that he cannot seize the property, making answer A incorrect.

General Police Duties, para. 3.2.8.1

107. Answer **D** — The Terrorism Act 2000, s. 33 states:
(1) An area is a cordoned area for the purposes of this Act if it is designated under this section.
(2) A designation may be made only if the person making it considers it expedient for the purposes of a terrorist investigation.

(3)   If a designation is made orally, the person making it shall confirm it in writing as soon as is reasonably practicable.

Section 33(3) states that the designation can be given orally (making answer C incorrect).

The Terrorism Act 2000, s. 34 states:

(1)   Subject to subsections (1A), (1B) and (2), a designation under section 33 may only be made—

   (a) where the area is outside Northern Ireland and is wholly or partly within a police area, by an officer for the police area who is of at least the rank of superintendent, and

   (b) ...

(1A) ...

(1B) ...

(1C) ...

(2)   A constable who is not of the rank required by subsection (1) may make a designation if he considers it necessary by reason of urgency.

(3)   Where a constable makes a designation in reliance on subsection (2) he shall as soon as is reasonably practicable—

   (a) make a written record of the time at which the designation was made, and

   (b) ensure that a police officer of at least the rank of superintendent is informed.

(4)   An officer who is informed of a designation in accordance with subsection (3)(b)—

   (a) shall confirm the designation or cancel it with effect from such time as he may direct, and

   (b) shall, if he cancels the designation, make a written record of the cancellation and the reason for it.

Section 34(1)(a) states that the designation will be normally be made by an officer who is of at least the rank of superintendent (making answers A and B incorrect). However, in an urgent situation a constable can make the designation (s. 34(2)). If that is the case, the officer will inform an officer of the rank of superintendent or above as soon as reasonably practicable.

General Police Duties, paras 3.15.7 to 3.15.7.2

108. Answer **A** — The Criminal Damage Act 1971, s. 1 states:

(1) A person who without lawful excuse destroys or damages any property belonging to another intending to destroy or damage any such property or being reckless as to whether any such property would be destroyed or damaged shall be guilty of an offence.

A person shall be treated as having lawful excuse under s. 5(2):

(a) if at the time of the act or acts alleged to constitute the offence he believed that the person or persons whom he believed to be entitled to consent to the destruction of or damage to the property in question had so consented, or would have so consented to it if he or they had known of the destruction or damage and its circumstances ...

That would be the case in respect of ORTEGA as s. 5(2)(a) would provide a statutory defence to any later charge of criminal damage by Amy SAMUELSON. The key element here would be that ORTEGA believed she had the consent of the owner of the TV (Kelly SAMUELSON and someone ORTEGA believes to be entitled to consent to that damage) to damage the TV in these circumstances. This makes answers B and C incorrect.

Section 10 of the Act deals with the 'belonging to another' phrase and states:

(2) Property shall be treated for the purposes of this Act as belonging to any person—
    (a) having the custody or control of it;
    (b) having in it any proprietary right or interest (not being an equitable interest arising only from an agreement to transfer or grant an interest); or
    (c) having a charge on it.

This extended meaning of 'belonging to another' is similar to that used in the Theft Act 1968. One result is that if a person damages their own property, they may still commit the offence of simple criminal damage if that property also 'belongs to' someone else. As Kelly knows this is the case, she could be charged with criminal damage (making answer C further incorrect). Answer D is incorrect as the Theft Act 1968 states that where the property in question belongs to D's spouse or civil partner, a prosecution for unlawful damage may only be instituted against D by or with the consent of the DPP (s. 30(4)). This restriction does not apply to other persons charged with committing the offence jointly with D; nor does it apply when the parties are separated by judicial decree or order or under no obligation to cohabit (s. 30(4)(a)).

Crime, paras 1.16.2 to 1.16.2.5

109. Answer **B** — Section 71(2) of the Domestic Abuse Act 2021 states that it is *not a defence* that the victim of a 'relevant offence' consented to the infliction of the serious harm for the purposes of obtaining sexual gratification. A 'relevant offence' means an offence under s. 18, 20 or 47 of the Offences Against the Person Act 1861.

'Serious harm' means:

- grievous bodily harm, within the meaning of s. 18 of the 1861 Act;
- wounding, within the meaning of that section, or
- actual bodily harm, within the meaning of s. 47 of the 1861 Act.

Section 71(2) would be relevant to all the offences committed but the question specifically asks at what point would that *first* be the case—that is when the s. 47 offence is committed (correct answer B).

EXCLUDED QUESTION, *Crime*, para. 1.10.5.3

110. Answer **D** — Unlike the other Fraud Act 2006 offences, the offence under s. 11 is not a conduct crime; it is a result crime and requires the actual obtaining of the service (answer A is incorrect). However, the offence does not require a fraudulent representation or deception (answer B is incorrect). Someone would commit this offence if, intending to avoid payment, he/she slipped into a concert hall to watch a concert without paying for the privilege. The offence can be committed where the defendant intends to avoid payment or payment in full but the defendant must know that the services are made available on the basis that they are chargeable, i.e. services provided for free are not covered by the offence.

If D sneaks aboard a lorry or a freight train and obtains a free ride, D would commit no offence under s. 11 because the haulage company or freight train operator does not provide such rides, even for payment (correct answer D—this also makes answer C incorrect).

Crime, para. 1.15.9

111. Answer **D** — In a case of simple criminal damage it may be relatively straightforward to prove a causal link between the actions of the defendant and the resulting crime: a defendant throws a brick at a window and the window is broken by the brick hitting it; the window would not have broken 'but for' the defendant's conduct. Where the link becomes more difficult to prove is when the defendant's behaviour triggers other events or aggravates existing circumstances. This MCQ is an example of such a situation and closely follows the circumstances of case law in the decision in *R* v *McKechnie* [1992] Crim LR 194. In that case, the defendant attacked the victim, who was already suffering from a serious ulcer, causing him brain damage. The brain damage (caused by the assault) prevented doctors from operating on the ulcer which eventually ruptured, killing the victim. The Court of Appeal, upholding the conviction for manslaughter, held that the defendant's criminal conduct (the assault) had made a significant contribution to the victim's death even though the untreated ulcer was the actual cause of death (correct answer D), therefore answers A and C are incorrect. Answer B is incorrect as the chain of causation can be broken, for example by an intervening act.

EXCLUDED QUESTION, *Crime*, para. 1.2.6

112. Answer **A** — The Public Order Act 1986, s. 38 states:

(1) It is an offence for a person, with the intention—
   (a) of causing public alarm or anxiety, or
   (b) of causing injury to members of the public consuming or using the goods, or
   (c) of causing economic loss to any person by reason of the goods being shunned by members of the public, or
   (d) of causing economic loss to any person by reason of steps taken to avoid any such alarm or anxiety, injury or loss,
   to contaminate or interfere with goods, or make it appear that goods have been contaminated or interfered with, or to place goods which have been contaminated or interfered with, or which appear to have been contaminated or interfered with in a place where goods of that description are consumed, used, sold or otherwise supplied.

(2) It is also an offence for a person, with any such intention as is mentioned in paragraph (a), (c) or (d) of subsection (1), to threaten that he or another will do, or to claim that he or another has done, any of the acts mentioned in that subsection.

(3) It is an offence for a person to be in possession of any of the following articles with a view to the commission of an offence under subsection (1)—
   (a) materials to be used for contaminating or interfering with goods or making it appear that goods have been contaminated or interfered with, or
   (b) goods which have been contaminated or interfered with, or which appear to have been contaminated or interfered with.

Section 38(3) would capture BUCKFIELD's activities when he purchases the needles in the craft shop (correct answer A). The fact that the actual contamination activity occurred at BUCKFIELD's home address is irrelevant and this would be an offence under s. 38(1) so answer B is incorrect. Answer C is incorrect as when BUCKFIELD places the apples in the computer games aisle an offence is committed under s. 38(1)—the reference to 'in a place' in s. 38(1) should not be interpreted restrictively and placing the apples in the computer games sections would be placing them '*in a place* where goods of that description are consumed, used, sold or otherwise supplied'. Answer D is incorrect as 'goods' includes 'natural' goods (e.g. fruit and vegetables) or 'manufactured' goods (e.g. shampoo or disinfectant)—contaminating 'manufactured' goods with the needles would be just as much an offence as contaminating the apples.

Crime, para. 1.16.7

113. Answer **D** — Section 15(7) of the Police and Criminal Evidence Act 1984 states that two copies shall be made of a warrant which specifies only one set of premises and does not authorise multiple entries; and as many copies as are reasonably required may be made of any other kind of warrant. This means that answers A, B and C are incorrect and that answer D is correct.

General Police Duties, para. 3.2.3.2

114. Answer **A** — The offence of aggravated burglary under s. 10 of the Theft Act is committed when a person commits a burglary (under s. 9(1)(a) or s. 9(1)(b)) and at the time has with him/her any firearm, imitation firearm, any weapon of offence or any explosive. A weapon of offence is any article made, adapted or intended to cause injury to another or to incapacitate another. A bayonet is a weapon of offence per se and the rope is a weapon of offence as KELT intends to use it to incapacitate a person. The phrase 'has with him' means 'immediate control of the item'. As KELT *knows* about the bayonet then he 'has it with him'. This means that CALDERDALE and KELT commit the offence in relation to the bayonet (answer D is incorrect) but only KELT in relation to the rope (making answers B and C incorrect and answer A correct).

Crime, paras 1.14.6 to 1.14.6.1

115. Answer **B** — Answer C is incorrect as s. 5(4) of the Misuse of Drugs Act 1971 is a defence to unlawful possession—it will not provide a defence to any other offence connected with the controlled drug (e.g. supplying or offering to supply). Answer D is incorrect as s. 28 is a general defence to a defendant charged with certain drugs offences. Section 28 applies to offences of:

- unlawful production (s. 4(2));
- unlawful supply (s. 4(3));
- unlawful possession (s. 5(2));
- possession with intent to supply (s. 5(3));
- unlawful cultivation of cannabis (s. 6(2));
- offences connected with opium (s. 9) (not covered in the NPPF Step 2 Exam syllabus).

The defences under s. 28 are *not* available in cases of conspiracy as conspiracy is not an offence under the 1971 Act (*R* v *McGowan* [1990] Crim LR 399). Answer A is incorrect as possession of drugs paraphernalia (e.g. clingfilm, contact details etc.) will be relevant evidence to show that a defendant was an active dealer in drugs but it does not prove the intention to supply (*R* v *Haye* [2002] EWCA Crim 2476). In proving an intention to supply, you may be able to adduce evidence of the defendant's unexplained wealth (*R* v *Smith (Ivor)*

[1995] Crim LR 940) or the presence of large sums of money with the drugs seized (*R v Wright* [1994] Crim LR 55) (correct answer B).

Crime, paras 1.6.3.8, 1.6.5, 1.6.9

116. Answer **C** — The Criminal Law Act 1967, s. 3(1) states:

A person may use such force as is reasonable in the circumstances in the prevention of crime or in effecting or assisting in the lawful arrest of offenders or suspected offenders or of persons unlawfully at large.

So the starting point is to say that the use of '*reasonable* force' in self-defence or the defence of another is acceptable.

Section 76 of the Criminal Justice and Immigration Act 2008 applies to s. 3(1) of the Criminal Law Act 1967, particularly to the question as to whether the degree of force used was reasonable in the circumstances. The 'degree of force' means the type and amount of force used. Section 76(10)(b) states that reasonable force in self-defence includes acting in the defence of another person. Answer B is incorrect as using force to defend another (GRAYSON's wife) is acceptable—the issue now becomes whether the degree of force used was acceptable.

The question whether the degree of force used by the defendant was reasonable in the circumstances is to be decided by reference to the circumstances *as the defendant believed them to be* (s. 76(3)). Section 76(6) adds that the degree of force used by the defendant is not to be regarded as reasonable in the circumstances as the defendant believed them to be if it was *disproportionate* in those circumstances.

At this stage, it might appear that the force used by GRAYSON was unacceptable if it were considered 'disproportionate' but s. 43 of the Crime and Courts Act 2013 amends s. 76 of the Criminal Justice and Immigration Act 2008 so that the use of *disproportionate* force can be regarded as reasonable in the circumstances as the accused believed them to be when *householders* are acting to protect themselves or others from trespassers in their homes (self-defence)—meaning that answer D is incorrect and that answer C is correct. The use of *grossly* disproportionate force would still not be permitted (making answer A incorrect).

Crime, paras 1.4.5.2 to 1.4.5.4

117. Answer **B** — Section 40 of the Police and Criminal Evidence Act 1984 sets out the times when reviews must be conducted. In the case of a person who has been arrested but not charged (LITTLE), the second review shall be not later than nine hours after the first. The first review was carried out at 14.00hrs that day so the second review shall not be later than nine hours after that (23.00hrs), making answers A, C and D incorrect.

Evidence and Procedure, para. 2.6.16.12

118. Answer **D** — Where a person is remanded in custody, it normally means detention in prison. However, s. 128 of the Magistrates' Courts Act 1980 provides that a magistrates' court may remand a person to police custody:

- for a period not exceeding three clear days (24 hours for persons under 18 (s. 91(5) of the Legal Aid, Sentencing and Punishment of Offenders Act 2012) (s. 128(7)); this makes answers B and C incorrect;

- for the purpose of enquiries into offences (other than the offence for which he/she appears before the court) (s. 128(8)(a)); this makes answer A incorrect;
- as soon as the need ceases, he/she must be brought back before the magistrates (s. 128(8)(b));
- the conditions of detention and periodic review apply as if the person was arrested without warrant on suspicion of having committed an offence (s. 128(8)(c) and (d)) (correct answer D).

Evidence and Procedure, para. 2.2.11

119. Answer **C** — Section 17(2) states that if a person, at the time of his committing or being arrested for an offence specified in sch. 1 to this Act, has in his possession a firearm or imitation firearm, he shall be guilty of an offence under this subsection unless he shows that he had it in his possession for a lawful object. The offence applies to firearms and imitation firearms (so both the rifle and the imitation revolver would be covered), meaning that answer A is incorrect. Child abduction under s. 2 of the Child Abduction Act 1984 is a sch. 1 offence, meaning that answer B is incorrect. It does not matter whether the person concerned is ultimately found guilty of the offence for which they were arrested, making answer D incorrect.

Crime, para. 1.7.11.5

120. Answer **C** — The Road Traffic Act 1988, s. 10 states:

(1) Subject to subsections (2) and (3) below, a person required under section 7 or 7A to provide a specimen of breath, blood or urine may afterwards be detained at a police station (or, if the specimen was provided otherwise than at a police station, arrested and taken to and detained at a police station) if a constable has reasonable grounds for believing that, were that person then driving or attempting to drive a mechanically propelled vehicle on a road, he would commit an offence under section 4, 5 or 5A of this Act.

The trigger for the power under s. 10 is that a person has been required to provide a specimen of breath, blood or urine under s. 7 or 7A of the Act—not that the offence was drug-related under s. 5A (meaning that answer D is incorrect). A consultation with a medical professional is required if the person's ability to drive properly is or might be impaired through drink or drugs—that is not the case here, making answer B incorrect. The power under s. 10 can be used if a constable believes (not suspects) that were that person then driving or attempting to drive (not just driving) a mechanically propelled vehicle on a road, he/she would commit an offence under s. 4, 5 or 5A (not just s. 5 or 5A)—the incorrect elements of answer A are in the brackets—answer C is therefore correct.

General Police Duties, para. 3.22.7

121. Answer **D** — Section 1 of the Road Traffic Act 1988 states that a person who causes the death of another person by driving a mechanically propelled vehicle dangerously on a road or other public place is guilty of an offence. As the incident occurred on private land, the offence has not been committed (correct answer D). This immediately makes answers A and C incorrect as they are 'Yes' options but, in addition, answer A is incorrect as the fact that a driver was adversely affected by alcohol is a circumstance relevant to the issue of dangerous driving, but **is not** in itself determinative to prove the offence (*R* v *Webster* [2006] 2 Cr App R 103). Answer C is incorrect as stated, however it is relevant to point out that where the defendant is

charged under s. 1, evidence of drink will be admissible where the quantity of it may have adversely affected the quality of the person's driving (*R v Woodward* [1995] RTR 130). Answer B states that the reason the offence has not been committed is that VIVIER was driving a mechanically propelled vehicle not a motor vehicle—but the offence relates to mechanically propelled vehicles (the fact that the 'Go-Ped' is actually a motor vehicle (*Chief Constable of North Yorkshire Police v Saddington* [2001] RTR 15) is therefore irrelevant).

General Police Duties, paras 3.19.5, 3.21.2

122. Answer **A** — There is nothing preventing a charge of 'attempted kidnap', meaning that answer D is incorrect. The 'taking or carrying away' need not involve a great distance, meaning answer C is incorrect. Answer B is incorrect as the taking or carrying away can be accomplished by force or by fraud. In *R v Hendy-Freegard* [2007] EWCA Crim 1236, the defendant was a confidence trickster who pretended to be an undercover agent working for MI5 or Scotland Yard. He would tell his victims that he was investigating the activities of the IRA and that his investigations had revealed that they were in danger. This allowed him to take control of their lives for a number of years and in doing so to direct them to move about the country from location to location. The defendant was eventually arrested and convicted of kidnapping on the basis of the Crown's case that the offence of kidnapping had occurred, as his victims had made journeys around the country which they had been induced to make as a result of the defendant's false story. The defendant successfully appealed against the kidnapping conviction, with the court stating that causing a person to move from place to place *when unaccompanied by the defendant* could not itself constitute either taking or carrying away or deprivation of liberty, which were necessary elements of the offence.

Crime, para. 1.11.3

123. Answer **B** — Answer C is incorrect as an authorisation under s. 47A of the Terrorism Act 2000 authorises any constable in uniform to stop a vehicle in the specified area or place and to search—

(a) the vehicle;
(b) the driver of the vehicle;
(c) a passenger in the vehicle;
(d) anything in or on the vehicle or carried by the driver or a passenger.

Answer D is incorrect as a constable in uniform may exercise the power conferred by an authorisation only for the purpose of discovering whether there is anything which may constitute evidence that the vehicle concerned is being used for the purposes of terrorism or (as the case may be) that the person concerned is a terrorist within the meaning of s. 40 (s. 47A(4)). However, the power conferred by such an authorisation may be exercised whether or not the constable reasonably suspects that there is such evidence (s. 47A(5)).

PC BUCHANAN correctly stopped the vehicle and also correctly arrested SNOOKS (answer A is incorrect, answer B is correct) as the Terrorism Act 2000, s. 41(1) states that a constable may arrest without a warrant a person whom he/she reasonably suspects to be a terrorist.

General Police Duties, paras 3.15.6.1, 3.15.6.4

124. Answer **D** — The Public Order Act 1986, s. 18 states:

(1) A person who uses threatening, abusive or insulting words or behaviour, or displays any written material which is threatening, abusive or insulting, is guilty of an offence if—
    (a) he intends thereby to stir up racial hatred, or
    (b) having regard to all the circumstances racial hatred is likely to be stirred up thereby.
(2) An offence under this section may be committed in a public or a private place, except that no offence is committed where the words or behaviour are used, or the written material is displayed, by a person inside a dwelling and are not heard or seen except by other persons in that or another dwelling [correct answer D].

Section 18(2) provides an exception to the offence, setting out circumstances where the offence *will not* be committed—this is the situation with BARTON—he *has not* committed the offence (answers A and C are incorrect). Answer B is incorrect as it can be committed by someone in a dwelling if the activity was heard or seen by a person who was not in the same dwelling or another one; for example, if a person walking on the street heard BARTON's language then the offence could be committed.

General Police Duties, para. 3.12.2.1

125. Answer **B** — Preliminary tests can be required and administered in a variety of circumstances.

Regardless of those circumstances, the officer *making the requirement* for the preliminary test to take place *does not have to be in uniform*—an officer in plain clothes can make the requirement which eliminates answers A and C. The officer administering a preliminary test (breath test, drug test or impairment test) must be in uniform (s. 6(7) of the Act); however, this uniform requirement only applies to preliminary tests administered under s. 6(2) to (4) of the Act—it does not apply in cases of preliminary tests following an accident (s. 6(5) of the Act). Section 6 of the Road Traffic Act 1988 states:

(5) This subsection applies if—
    (a) an accident occurs owing to the presence of a motor vehicle on a road or other public place, and
    (b) a constable reasonably believes that the person was driving, attempting to drive or in charge of the vehicle at the time of the accident.

There is no need for the police officer making the requirement to believe or even suspect that the person has been drinking, or that he/she has committed any offence; reasonable belief in his/her involvement (as a person driving, attempting to drive or being in charge of a vehicle) in the accident is enough. There is also no need for the officer administering the test to be in uniform, making answer D incorrect.

General Police Duties, paras 3.22.4 to 3.22.4.3

126. Answer **B** — The Theft Act 1968, s. 17 states:

(1) Where a person dishonestly, with a view to gain for himself or another or with intent to cause loss to another,—
    (a) destroys, defaces, conceals or falsifies any account or any record or document made or required for any accounting purpose; or

(b) in furnishing information for any purpose produces or makes use of any account, or any such record or document as aforesaid, which to his knowledge is or may be misleading, false or deceptive in a material particular;

he shall [commit an offence].

Answer A is incorrect as this is an 'intention' offence and no result is required—the fact that there was actually no loss or gain is immaterial. Answer C is incorrect as the offence can be committed in a number of ways which would include falsification of an account etc. and also omissions. Answer D is incorrect as there is no requirement to prove an intention permanently to deprive. Answer B is correct as an application for a mortgage or a loan to a commercial institution is a document required for an accounting purpose, the rationale being that applications for a mortgage or a loan to commercial institutions will, if successful, lead to the opening of an account which will show as credits in favour of the borrower any funds received from the borrower and will show as debits paid out by the lender to, or on behalf of, the borrower (*R v O and H* [2010] EWCA Crim 2233).

EXCLUDED QUESTION, *Crime*, para. 1.15.10

127. Answer **D** — Part 3 of the Anti-social Behaviour, Crime and Policing Act 2014 provides a dispersal power enabling officers (constables in uniform and police community support officers (PCSOs)) to direct a person who has committed, or is likely to commit, anti-social behaviour to leave a specified area and not return for a specified period of up to 48 hours (answers B and C are therefore incorrect). Answer A is incorrect as the direction would in most instances be given in writing to ensure that those individuals being dispersed are clear where they are being dispersed from. Where this is not reasonably practicable, *the direction could be given orally* (s. 35(5)(a)) and the officer would keep a written record of the direction (s. 38). The dispersal power can only be used where an officer of at least the rank of inspector has authorised its use in a specified locality (s. 34(1)). That authorisation can only be given where the police officer of or above the rank of inspector reasonably believes that, in respect of any locality within their police area, the exercise of the dispersal powers in part 3 of the Act may be required in order to remove or reduce the likelihood of the anti-social behaviour occurring (correct answer D).

General Police Duties, paras 3.7.5 to 3.7.5.1

128. Answer **A** — Nobody is saying that WHYTE is guilty of an offence at this stage—this question simply asks 'Is he in possession of the cocaine?' and the answer is 'Yes' (answer A) because possession is a neutral concept, not implying any fault, blame or guilt. To be in 'possession' of something, the person needs to have custody/control of it and to know that the thing in question is under his/her control (making answer C incorrect). WHYTE knows he has custody/control over the envelope so he possesses it. It does not matter that he thinks it contains £200 cash or that he did not know that it contained cocaine (answers B and D)—he knew it contained something so he is therefore in possession of that something.

Crime, paras 1.6.3 to 1.6.3.2

129. Answer **C** — The right of a detained person to have someone informed of their whereabouts can be delayed if an officer of the rank of inspector or above authorises it, making answers B and D incorrect. The right cannot be delayed beyond 36 hours after the relevant time, making answer A incorrect.

Evidence and Procedure, paras 2.6.9. to 2.6.9.1, 2.6.20

130. Answer **C** — Answer A is incorrect as Professional Standards Departments (PSDs) have final responsibility for the value judgement on whether information relating to misconduct of police officers should be revealed to the prosecutor. Answer D is incorrect as not only might the credibility of witnesses undermine the prosecution case, but so too might complaints against officers involved in the case, together with any occasions where officers have not been believed in court in the past. In these cases, it will be necessary to decide whether this information should be disclosed to the defence and, if disclosed, in how much detail. Advice given to prosecutors can assist when considering complaints and misconduct of police officers. The advice states:

It is, of course, necessary in the first instance for the police to bring such matters to the notice of the prosecutor, but it is submitted that the prosecutor should have a greater element of discretion than with the disclosure of previous convictions. With convictions against prosecution witnesses, disclosure normally follows, whereas in relation to disciplinary findings regard should be had to the nature of the finding and its likely relevance to the matters in issue. Findings which involve some element of dishonesty should invariably be disclosed, while matters such as disobedience to orders, neglect of duty and discreditable conduct will often have no relevance to the officer's veracity or the guilt or otherwise of a defendant. Certainly, there should be no duty on the prosecution to disclose details of unsubstantiated complaints even though this is a popular type of inquiry from some defence representatives. The imposition of such a duty would only encourage the making of false complaints in the hope that they might be used to discredit an officer in the future.

There is no absolute requirement to disclose findings in relation to disciplinary matters (answer B is incorrect). Answer C is correct as per the above passage of text.

Evidence and Procedure, para. 2.5.6.5

131. Answer **C** — The Criminal Attempts Act 1981 tells us that an attempt is an action that is 'more than merely preparatory' to the commission of an offence. Buying the materials to make a petrol bomb and walking over to MORRITT's house are merely preparatory (answers A and B are incorrect). Liability comes about at point C where CUNLIFFE tries to commit the offence of arson (correct answer C and this makes answer D incorrect). The fact that the petrol bomb does not ignite is immaterial—if it did, this would amount to the substantive offence of arson.

Crime, para. 1.3.4

132. Answer **A** — The Police and Criminal Evidence Act 1984, s. 80 states:

(2A) In any proceedings the spouse or civil partner of a person charged in the proceedings shall, subject to subsection (4) below, be compellable—
    (a) to give evidence on behalf of any other person charged in the proceedings but only in respect of any specified offence with which that other person is charged; or

(b) to give evidence for the **prosecution** but only in respect of any **specified offence** with which any person is charged in the proceedings.

(3) In relation to the spouse or civil partner of a person charged in any proceedings, an offence is a specified offence for the purposes of subsection (2A) above if—

(a) it involves an assault on, or injury or a threat of injury to, the spouse or civil partner or a person who was at the material time under the age of 16;

(b) it is a sexual offence alleged to have been committed in respect of a person who was at the material time under that age; or

(c) it consists of attempting or conspiring to commit, or of aiding, abetting, counselling, procuring or inciting the commission of, an offence falling within paragraph (a) or (b) above.

The law in s. 80(2A) means that answer D is incorrect as a wife can be a compellable witness against her husband in relation to certain offences. Answer C is incorrect as the offence of murder in not contained in s. 80(3). In this situation, Felicity ABBOTT would not be a compellable witness. However, there is no requirement to tell a wife that she is not a compellable witness against her husband before interviewing her about a crime of which her husband is suspected (answer B is incorrect). A statement obtained from the wife in such circumstances could be admitted in evidence even though the wife refused to give evidence against her husband, provided it did not lead to an injustice (*R v L* [2008] EWCA Crim 973) (correct answer A).

Evidence and Procedure, para. 2.3.7.5

133. Answer **C** — A person who without lawful excuse destroys or damages any property belonging to another intending to destroy or damage such property or being reckless as to whether any such property will be damaged or destroyed commits an offence of criminal damage (s. 1(1) of the Criminal Damage Act 1971). 'Property' includes money which makes answer B incorrect. The property must 'belong to another' and as the shirts belong to ROUGHTON (they were given to him as a gift), then he cannot commit the s. 1(1) offence in relation to them meaning that answer A is incorrect. However, it is possible for a person to commit criminal damage to his/her own property if it also belongs to someone else (e.g. the property in question is jointly owned). As the money belongs to ROUGHTON and to CRANE then ROUGHTON can damage it, meaning that answer D is incorrect and answer C is correct.

Crime, paras 1.16.2 to 1.16.2.3

134. Answer **A** — Whether or not a defendant is legally represented in an interview will not prevent adverse inferences being drawn (unless the defendant is being held incommunicado and legal advice has been withheld after the defendant has requested a solicitor), making answer D incorrect. A defendant cannot be convicted solely on an adverse inference drawn from silence, making answer B incorrect. Adverse inferences can be drawn from an interview where the suspect remains silent, responds 'no comment' to questioning or fails to mention any fact relied on in their defence in proceedings, making answer C incorrect.

Evidence and Procedure, para. 2.8.2.3

135. Answer **D** — Section 18 of the Police and Criminal Evidence Act 1984 states:

(1) Subject to the following provisions of this section, a constable may enter and search any premises occupied or controlled by a person who is under arrest for an indictable offence, if he has reasonable grounds for *suspecting* that there is on the premises evidence, other than items subject to legal privilege, that relates—
(a) to that offence; or
(b) to some other indictable offence which is connected with or similar to that offence.
(2) A constable may seize and retain anything for which he may search under subsection (1) above.
(3) The power to search conferred by subsection (1) above is only a power to search to the extent that is reasonably required for the purpose of discovering such evidence.
(4) Subject to subsection (5) below, the powers conferred by this section may not be exercised unless an officer of the rank of inspector or above has *authorised them in writing*.

The search takes place if the officer has reasonable grounds for suspecting (not believing), eliminating answers B and C. An inspector must provide his/her written authorisation, making answer A incorrect.

General Police Duties, para. 3.2.5.3

136. Answer **A** — Answers B and D are incorrect as a direction under s. 42 cannot be given as the Criminal Justice and Police Act 2001 gives the police specific powers to prevent the intimidation or harassment of people in *their own or others' homes* (correct answer A). Answer B is further incorrect as the direction does not have to be given by an officer in uniform. The direction is given by the most senior ranking police officer at the scene, making answer C incorrect.

General Police Duties, para. 3.12.7

137. Answer **A** — Answer B is incorrect as you cannot attempt to commit a summary only offence and a s. 39 assault/battery is a summary only offence. Answer C is incorrect as HATTON did not intend to cause grievous bodily harm to any person. Answer D is incorrect as the state of mind required for one offence can, on occasions, be 'transferred' from the original target or victim to another. *This only operates if the crime remains the same.* In other words, a defendant cannot be convicted if he/she acted with the *mens rea* for one offence but commits the *actus reus* of another offence. In *R* v *Latimer* (1886) 17 QBD 359, the defendant lashed out with his belt at one person but missed, striking a third party instead. As it was proved that the defendant had the required *mens rea* when he swung the belt, the court held that the same *mens rea* could support a charge of wounding against any other victim injured by the same act. If the *nature of the offence* changes, then this approach will not operate. Therefore if a defendant is shown to have thrown a rock at a crowd of people intending to injure one of them, the *mens rea* required for that offence cannot be 'transferred' to an offence of criminal damage if the rock misses that person and breaks a window instead (*R* v *Pembliton* (1874) LR 2 CCR 119). The state of mind required for an offence under s. 20 of the Offences Against the Person Act 1861 is 'maliciousness' (recklessness) that 'some harm' will befall someone—that is exactly what has occurred here so HATTON is liable for the s. 20 offence against OGDEN. No contact is required for an assault at a s. 39 level—just the apprehension of immediate unlawful violence (correct answer A).

Crime, paras 1.1.11, 1.3.4, 1.10.7 to 1.10.7.5

138. Answer **D** — Section 7(2) of the Road Traffic Act 1988 states that a requirement under s. 7 to provide evidential breath specimens can be made:

(a) at a police station;

(b) at a hospital; or

(c) at or near a place where a preliminary breath test has been administered to that person or would have been but for his/her failure to cooperate with it.

The requirement for the specimen can be made at any of these locations (meaning that answers A and B are incorrect); 'other medical premises' are not included in s. 7(2) meaning that answer C is incorrect.

General Police Duties, para. 3.22.5.2

139. Answer **B** — Answer A is incorrect as an adult may be removed to, kept at or taken to a place of safety that is a police station but only in circumstances specified in the Mental Health Act 1983 (Places of Safety) Regulations 2017 (SI 2017/1036). Regulation 2 provides that a police station can only be used as a place of safety for an adult where the person exercising, or authorising the exercise of, the power under s. 135 or s. 136 is satisfied that:

(a) the behaviour of the adult presents an imminent risk of serious injury or death to that adult or to others;

(b) as a result, no other place of safety in the police area in which the adult is located can reasonably be expected to detain them; and

(c) the adult will have access to a health-care professional, so far as is reasonably practicable, throughout the period in which they are detained at the police station.

Regulation 2 further provides that where the person considering using a police station as a place of safety is a police officer, they must, if reasonably practicable, consult with a registered medical practitioner, a registered nurse, an approved mental health professional, an occupational therapist or a paramedic before making the decision. The decision to use a police station as a place of safety must be authorised by an officer of the rank of inspector or above (correct answer B). Answer D is incorrect as anyone being taken to a place of safety or detained at such a place will be treated as being in legal custody (s. 137(1)). This expression is only relevant in relation to escaping and assisting in an escape; it is very different from 'in police detention' used under s. 118 of the Police and Criminal Evidence Act 1984.

Answer C is incorrect as a person removed to or kept at a place of safety under this section may be detained there for the permitted period of detention for the purpose of enabling him/her to be examined by a registered medical practitioner and to be interviewed by an approved mental health professional and of making any necessary arrangements for his/her treatment or care. The Mental Health Act 1983, s. 136 states:

(2A) In subsection (2), 'the permitted period of detention' means—

(a) the period of 24 hours beginning with—

(i) in a case where the person is removed to a place of safety, the time when the person arrives at that place;

> (ii) in a case where the person is kept at a place of safety, the time when the constable decides to keep the person at that place; or
>
> (b) where an authorisation is given in relation to the person under section 136B, that period of 24 hours and such further period as is specified in the authorisation.

EXCLUDED QUESTION, General Police Duties, para. 3.4.2

140. Answer **D** — The basic period of detention is 24 hours. This can be extended by a superintendent to 36 hours. After this, a warrant of further detention can extend the detention for another 36 hours. Further applications can be made by the police and detention can be extended up to a maximum total of 96 hours.

Evidence and Procedure, paras 2.6.16.3, 2.6.16.7

141. Answer **D** — Code A of the Codes of Practice applies to all powers of stop and search requiring 'reasonable grounds to suspect' as a basis for the search and therefore applies to a search carried out under s. 1 of the Police and Criminal Evidence Act 1984. Code A states that the searching officer can, in public view:

- place his/her hands inside the pockets of outer clothing (so there is nothing wrong with PC CULPAN doing this to FRASER, making answer A incorrect);
- feel round the inside of collars, socks and shoes (para. 3.5);
- search a person's hair, if this does not require the removal of headgear (para. 3.5);
- require the person to remove his/her outer coat, jacket and gloves.

The person *cannot* be required to remove any further clothing in public, but can be asked to remove more clothing voluntarily. If a more thorough search is required, this can be conducted but this must be out of public view, for example in a police van or at a nearby police station, making answer B incorrect. If the search involves removing anything beyond an outer coat, jacket, gloves, headgear or footwear, the searching officer and any other officers present must be of *the same sex* as the person being searched unless the person specifically requests otherwise. This is not the case inside the police van so the search in these circumstances was correct (making answer C incorrect).

EXCLUDED QUESTION, General Police Duties, para. 3.1.5

142. Answer **B** — Section 55A of PACE allows a person who has been arrested and is in police detention to have an X-ray taken of them or an ultrasound scan to be carried out on them (or both) if:

(a) authorised by an officer of inspector rank or above who has reasonable grounds for believing that the detainee:
  (i) may have swallowed a Class A drug; and
  (ii) was in possession of that Class A drug with the intention of supplying it to another or to export; and
(b) the detainee's appropriate consent has been given in writing.

Cannabis resin is a Class B drug so an X-ray or ultrasound scan could not be carried out in these circumstances, making answers A, C and D incorrect.

Evidence and Procedure, para. 2.6.25

143. Answer **C** — Where a court:

- has convicted a person of a drug trafficking offence; and
- it has determined that a sentence of four years or more is appropriate (correct answer C);

it is under a *duty* to consider whether or not a travel restriction order would be appropriate (s. 33 of the Criminal Justice and Police Act 2001). Answer A is incorrect as a 'drug trafficking offence' is defined by s. 34 of the Act and includes the production of a controlled drug (s. 4(2)), the supply of a controlled drug (s. 4(3)) and the importation/exportation offences under s. 3 along with inciting a person to commit these offences under s. 19 of the Misuse of Drugs Act 1971. It also includes aiding, abetting, counselling or procuring these offences. Answers B and D are incorrect as the order cannot be imposed but also because travel restriction orders prohibit offenders from leaving the United Kingdom at any time during the period beginning from their release from custody (other than on bail or temporary release for a fixed period) and up to the end of the order. The minimum period for such an order is two years (s. 33(3)); there is no maximum period prescribed in the legislation (making answer B further incorrect) and an offender may apply to the court that made a restriction order to have it revoked or suspended (s. 35). The court must consider the strict criteria set out in s. 35 when considering any such suspension or revocation. If an order is suspended, the offender has a legal obligation to be back in the United Kingdom when the period of suspension ends (s. 35(5)(a)) (making answer D further incorrect).

Crime, para. 1.6.16

144. Answer **B** — When an authorisation under s. 60 of the Criminal Justice and Public Order Act 1994 is given, you automatically get the powers provided by s. 60AA. So in addition to s. 60 powers, such an authorisation also allows officers *in uniform* to require any individual to remove any item (e.g. clothing, mask, scarf) if the officer reasonably believes that the person is wearing it/will wear it wholly or mainly to conceal his/her identity (this makes answers A and D incorrect). It is an offence to fail to remove such items when required to do so (s. 60AA(7)).

Therefore, PC MAKIN could use the power (making answer C incorrect). Note that this is not a power to stop and search a person for items that could be used to conceal their identity; it is only a power to stop a person and make the requirement to remove the item (making answer D further incorrect).

General Police Duties, paras 3.1.4.8 to 3.1.4.14

145. Answer **C** — The suspect is not allowed to be present when the images are shown to an eye-witness, making answer A incorrect. Answer B is incorrect as although the solicitor is not allowed to communicate with the witness, he/she would be allowed to communicate with the identification officer. A supervised viewing of the recording of the video identification procedure by the suspect and/or their solicitor may be arranged on request, at the discretion of the investigating officer not the identification officer, making answer D incorrect. Answer C is correct as a suspect's solicitor may only be present at the video identification on request and with the prior agreement of the identification officer, if the officer is satisfied that the solicitor's presence will not deter or distract any eye-witness from viewing the images and making an identification.

Evidence and Procedure, para. 2.7.8

146. Answer **A** — The offence of engaging in sexual activity in a public lavatory is committed when a person is in a lavatory to which the public or a section of the public has or is permitted to have access, whether on payment or otherwise (making answer B incorrect) and the person intentionally engages in an activity and that activity is sexual. Whether ROE can be seen by anyone else is immaterial, making answer C incorrect. The activity does not have to take place with another, making answer D incorrect.

Crime, para. 1.12.8.3

147. Answer **C** — The fact that TUCKWELL has provided two specimens of breath does not mean that he cannot be requested to supply a specimen of blood or urine for analysis (s. 7(3) of the Act), making answer B incorrect. A specimen of urine shall be provided within ONE hour of the requirement, making answer A incorrect. The requirement for a specimen of blood or urine can be made at a police station if the suspected offence is one under s. 3A or 4 of the Act and the constable making the request has been advised by a medical practitioner that the condition of the person required to provide the specimen might be due to some drug (s. 7(3)(c)), making answer D incorrect and answer C correct.

General Police Duties, para. 3.22.5.1

148. Answer **C** — The Bail Act 1976, s. 6 creates two offences in relation to absconding and states:

(1) If a person who has been released on bail in criminal proceedings fails without reasonable cause to surrender to custody he shall be guilty of an offence.
(2) If a person who—
   (a) has been released on bail in criminal proceedings, and
   (b) having reasonable cause therefor, has failed to surrender to custody,

fails to surrender to custody at the appointed place as soon after the appointed time as is reasonably practicable he shall be guilty of an offence.

Answer B is incorrect as s. 6 applies where:
- the police grant bail to a suspect to appear at the police station;
- the police grant bail to a defendant to appear at court on the first appearance;
- the court grants bail to the defendant to return to court at a later date.

Answer B is further incorrect as in *Laidlaw* v *Atkinson* (1986) The Times, 2 August, it was held that being mistaken about the day on which one should have appeared was not a reasonable excuse. Answer D is incorrect as failure to give to a person granted bail in criminal proceedings a copy of the record of the decision does not constitute reasonable cause for that person's failure to surrender to custody (s. 6(4)). As these are not 'reasonable excuses', this makes answer C correct.

Evidence and Procedure, para. 2.2.10

149. Answer **B** — Paragraph 16.5 of Code C states that a detainee may not be interviewed about an offence after they have been charged with it, or informed that they may be prosecuted for it, unless the interview is necessary:
- to prevent or minimise harm or loss to some other person, or the public;
- to clear up an ambiguity in a previous answer or statement;

- in the interests of justice for the detainee to have put to them, and have an opportunity to comment on, information concerning the offence which has come to light since they were charged or informed that they might be prosecuted.

The fact that such an interview can take place means that answers A and C are incorrect. You would not require the authority/permission of an officer of the rank of superintendent or above to carry out such an interview, meaning that answer D is incorrect.

Evidence and Procedure, para. 2.6.17

150. Answer **D** — The question as to whether or not sureties are necessary is at the discretion of the custody officer (or court) which makes answer C incorrect. Answer A is incorrect as s. 8(1) states that this section applies where a person is granted bail in criminal proceedings on condition that they provide *one or more surety or sureties* for the purpose of securing that they surrender to custody. It is not necessary to prove that the surety had any involvement in the accused's non-appearance (*R* v *Warwick Crown Court, ex parte Smalley* [1987] 1 WLR 237), making answer B incorrect. Answer D is the correct answer as s. 8(2) states that in considering the suitability for that purpose of a proposed surety, regard may be had (amongst other things) to:

(a) the surety's financial resources;
(b) his character and any previous convictions of his; and
(c) his proximity (whether in point of kinship, place of residence or otherwise) to the person for whom he is to be surety.

Evidence and Procedure, para. 2.2.7.4